- ✓ **Unlock your dog's potential**
- ✓ **Use positive methods**
- ✓ **How your dog learns**
- ✓ **Be the pack leader**

Julia Barnes

DOG
TRAINING
made easy

DEDICATION

In memory of Bruce, a fantastic dog.

THE QUESTION OF GENDER
The 'he' pronoun is used throughout this book instead of the rather impersonal 'it', but no gender bias is intended.

Originally published in 2009 by
The Pet Book Publishing Company
as *The Mini Encyclopaedia of Dog Training*

This revised edition first published 2011.
Reprinted 2012, 2013, 2014 and 2015 by
The Pet Book Publishing Company Limited
St Martin's Farm, Chapel Lane, Zeals,
Wiltshire BA12 6NZ.

ISBN
978-1-906305-52-9
1-906305-52-8

Printed by Printworks Global Ltd. , London & Hong Kong

CONTENTS

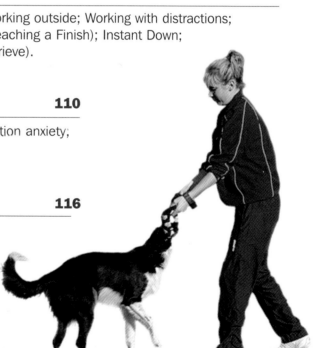

UNDERSTANDING DOGS

Chapter 1

We all love our dogs and celebrate their individual personalities. But a dog is so much more lovable when he is well behaved, co-operative and ready to fit in with your life. The aim is to have a dog to be proud of, not just because he looks noble or because he is sweet and cuddly, but because he is a pleasure to own.

TRACING BACK

There are hundreds of dog breeds to chose from, ranging from the tiny Chihuahua to the massive Irish Wolfhound. But they all trace their roots back to the wolf. This may seem irrelevant to modern-day dog owners, but, in fact, it is of immense significance.

The wolf lives in a pack, and

Wolves live in packs and will bond closely with pack members.

although it is more than 14,000 years since the first wolves joined the family circle and became domesticated, the dogs we own today still show behaviour that stems from living in a pack.

In a wolf pack, there is an established hierarchy, which means that the top- ranking dogs are the strongest and fittest, and will be the decision makers for the whole pack. They will lead the hunt and get the pick of any prey that is killed. But there will be plenty left for the lower-ranking pack mothers, and for cubs that are too young to hunt. If an enemy approaches, it is the top-ranking dogs that will fight in order to defend the pack and its established territory. The top-ranking (alpha) male and the top-ranking (alpha) female will breed, so that the very best genes

available will be passed on to the next generation.

Try to imagine what would happen if there was no leadership in the pack. The wolves would fail to co-operate when they were hunting, which would reduce the chances of success. They would squabble amongst themselves when they were sharing food, and would not provide for the younger, weaker pack members. There would be no strategy for defending the pack or for deciding when to move to fresh hunting grounds. If all this were not bad enough, there would be serious fighting among the males every time a female was ready for mating.

It is therefore obvious why certain species of animals opt to live in packs. A pack that is united behind a strong leader will thrive, and, more importantly, survive. There

may be a challenge to the leadership if a top-ranking animal starts to lose his powers, but, in general, all pack members accept the status quo and will be content with their position in the pack hierarchy.

BECOMING THE LEADER

We are incredibly lucky that the domesticated dog is still governed by a pack mentality. In fact, it is the reason why dogs are outstandingly successful as companions and helpmates. A dog's principal aim is to find his place in the pack because this ensures that his needs will be answered. When a puppy arrives in his new home and is introduced into the family circle, he needs to know who is going to provide his food, who is going to care for him, and who is going to make the decisions. The answer is you. This does not mean that you are the 'boss', strutting your stuff and making the puppy's life a misery. It means that you are his leader and you will make the decisions that will ensure his wellbeing.

WHAT MAKES A GOOD LEADER?
There are a number of factors that come into play. You need to be:

- **A provider:** A dog needs to understand that the quality of his life depends on you. You give him food, shelter, and the things he likes, such as play and exercise. In a dog's eyes, this is worthy of the highest respect.
- **A teacher:** A dog needs to understand what is required of him and be happy to co-operate.

You need to be firm in setting boundaries and consistent so that he always understands what you want of him.

- **A companion:** A dog should want nothing more than to be in your company, where he feels safe and secure. He is content and relaxed because he accepts your role as decision-maker.

WHAT MAKES A BAD LEADER?
Adopting the role as leader is not difficult, but some people struggle with the concept – and, more often than not, they end up with problem dogs. What are the most common mistakes that people make when failing to assume strong leadership?

- **Indecision:** If you cannot decide what your dog is and is not allowed to do, how is he supposed to know?
- **Pampering:** If you treat your dog like a beloved child, indulging him in everything you think he wants, he will lose his respect for you.
- **Weakness:** If you start letting your dog get away with undesirable behaviour because you don't want to have the battle, he will be swift to take advantage.

Essentially, a dog wants to please, and if you cut a convincing figure as his leader, he will see no need to challenge you.

THE DOG'S MIND
We all love to boast about how clever our dogs are, and we marvel at the top competitors in

The aim of every dog is to find a leader who will be both provider and decision-maker.

obedience, agility and the other canine sports, but even if you have modest ambitions, you need to understand how a dog's mind works in order to train him.

A dog has two ways of learning:

CONSEQUENCE LEARNING

A dog learns that specific behaviours produce specific consequences, i.e. cause and effect. As long as the consequence is immediate or closely linked, the dog will quickly learn if an action has a bad consequence or a good consequence.

ASSOCIATION LEARNING

This is when behaviour is triggered by association. For example, the first time a dog sees a lead, it means nothing to him. But when you clip the lead on and take him for a walk, he will start to associate the lead with being taken out. Soon the dog will see his lead and get excited because he knows it means he is going for a walk. In the same way, a dog will learn by negative association. If a dog has been ill treated and beaten with a stick, he only has to see a stick and he will become frightened and fearful.

TRAINING METHODS

We can make use of both consequence learning and association learning when we are training our dogs. As we have seen, the dog learns as a result of good and bad consequences, and good or bad associations. This

can be divided into:

- **Positive training:** Reward-based training methods, using treats and play as training aids, promoting a positive response. The dog wants to do as you ask because he can see an immediate reward for his 'good' behaviour.
- **Negative training:** A dog does as you ask because he is scared

of you and fears the consequences of his 'bad' behaviour.

It does not take a genius to work out which method is more likely to pay dividends. The aim is to have an eager, willing pupil who loves his training sessions because he gets lots of rewards, as well as the best reward of all – being with you.

A dog co-operates because he has learnt that pleasing you will reap rewards.

MEETING AND GREETING
A playful outcome

The dog (pictured right) is bold and confident, but the bitch is a little unsure.

The dog (right) goes into a bow position, inviting the bitch to play.

BODY LANGUAGE

As well as understanding how your dog's mind works, you need to be able to read his body language so that you know what he is feeling, and what his intentions might be. If you look at two dogs meeting each other, you will often see a variety of postures as the two dogs size each other up.

These are the most common ways that a dog expresses himself:

- Standing tall, with ears pricked, and a tail waving from side to side: This is an open, friendly stance, which shows a confident dog that has nothing to fear.
- An upright stance, alert expression, hackles lifted, and a stiff, upright tail: This dog is

worried and attempting to look big and bold. He may show aggressive behaviour, but this tends to be prompted by nervousness.

- An upright stance, accompanied by a hard stare, and lips curling back: This dog means business and is appearing dominant and assertive.

MEETING AND GREETING
The safe option

The standing dog asserts his authority while the other is crouching low to the ground to show he accepts his inferior status.

Gaining confidence, the dominant dog stands over the submissive one.

In this scenario, total submission is the safest option.

- A crouched body posture with ears flattened and tail between the legs: A nervous dog who is trying to appear as non-threatening as possible. This behaviour may well be followed up with the dog rolling on to his back in total submission.

A dog will also read your body language to understand your intentions. In fact, many dogs rely more on our body language than on the verbal commands or cues we give (see page 33).

VERBAL COMMUNICATION

Words are so important to us, but dogs will rely more on their own body language to communicate. The sounds most commonly made are:

- **BARKING:** This can range from a deep warning bark, signalling the approach of strangers, to an excited 'yip' to greet you when you come through the door. Some dogs will also bark as a sign of frustration if, for example, they are failing to understand what is required of them. If a dog is left for long periods on his own, he will develop a habit of barking to ease the boredom.
- **WHIMPERING:** This is a sound you would associate with young puppies telling their mother they are cold or hungry. An older dog may whimper if he is similarly distressed or uncomfortable.
- **WHINING:** This may be a sign of discomfort or pain. It can also be an attention-seeking device. A puppy spending his first night

on his own will often switch up the volume of his whines so they become ear splitting.
- **GROWLING:** This is a low sound coming from deep in the throat. It is a warning, signalling that aggressive, assertive behaviour will follow unless the growling is heeded.
- **SNARLING:** This is accompanied with lips curling back and will be followed up with an attack unless the situation changes.
- **HOWLING:** This is a throwback to the dog's wolf ancestry and may be triggered by an unusual sound or by hearing other dogs barking.
- **HIGH-PITCHED SCREAMING:** Hopefully, you will never hear this. It is induced by extreme pain or fear.

Puppies will whimper if they are cold or hungry.

Most dogs will give a warning bark when strangers approach their home territory. A dog may howl when he is on his own – but more often it is a group activity.

A dog is quick to learn verbal cues from his human family, and some highly trained dogs will progress to learning an extended vocabulary, responding to several dozen different commands.

However, all dogs will pick up on tone of voice as a key to understanding what we want, and this can be a very useful training tool (see page 36).

THE SENSES

We tend to think that dogs see the world exactly as we do, but, in fact, there are significant differences in our senses. It helps to be aware of these when you are training your dog, so you can work to his strengths.

THE POWER OF SCENT

A dog's sense of smell is reckoned to be 1,000 times better than a human's, which is why we struggle to understand why a dog finds sniffing a lamppost such a fascinating occupation.

While the human sense of smell is a useful tool, for a dog the ability to scent is of vital importance. A dog uses his sense of smell to find food, and he also uses it to pick up all the local

When eyes are set wide apart, it gives a broader field of vision.

news. Dogs scent mark, leaving their own personal ID, so when another dog investigates, he will know who has come calling. It could be a dog he knows, it could be a bitch in season, or it could be a stranger, posing a potential threat.

So when your dog is preoccupied with sniffing what appears to be a bare patch of grass, remember that he is absorbing a wealth of information.

SIGHT

Most dogs have eyes that are set wide apart to give a broad field of vision. Picking up details can be a struggle, but dogs are brilliant at detecting a moving object at a considerable distance. This goes back to the dog's hunting days when the slightest movement might indicate potential prey. Dogs have good night vision, but they do not see colours well. It is thought that they see the world in a range of purples, violets and yellows.

HEARING

An acute sense of hearing ensured survival in the wild. Danger, generally in the form of predators, could be heard long before it was sighted. A human can hear and

The dog's sense of smell is so strong, it can sense odours at concentrations 100 million times lower than we can.

interpret sound at a distance of 20 metres, while a dog can pick up sounds at a distance of some 80 metres. A dog can also move his ears in different directions, which helps him to pinpoint sound accurately. Sounds are transmitted at a range of frequencies and dogs have an exceptional ability to pick up sounds at ultra-high frequencies that we cannot hear at all.

SUMMING UP

The key to having a dog that is a perfect companion is to understand his needs and to tune into how his mind works.

If you can get on your dog's wavelength – and you can communicate with him in a way that he understands – you will build a deep and lasting relationship that will enrich both your life and his.

An acute sense of hearing means that a dog can give an early warning if he hears something that sounds suspicious.

A dog will move his ears as he tries to locate a sound.

WHAT CAN YOU EXPECT FROM YOUR DOG?

Chapter 2

We now have a good understanding of how a dog sees the world and how his mind works. Next we need to look at the huge range of dog breeds and find out how they differ from each other. Obviously, we can see that some breeds contrast dramatically in looks. For example, a Cavalier King Charles Spaniel and a Mastiff bear little or no resemblance to each other. But is the difference between them purely cosmetic? To answer this question we need to find out why different breeds were created.

When wolves were first domesticated, they found a place in the family circle, helping with the hunt and guarding the home. Some may have shown an aptitude for protecting livestock and herding it to new pastures, while others may have become expert in keeping down vermin such as rats and mice. If you want a dog to do a particular task, it makes sense to use the very best dogs available for breeding so that you produce dogs that are likely to excel in their chosen role.

The biggest, fiercest dogs would, therefore, be bred to produce impressive guards, the dogs with the best scenting ability would be bred to produce top-class hunting dogs, and the dogs who used their initiative to herd and drive livestock would be bred to work as shepherd dogs. This is how the first purebred dogs were produced, and some of our breeds date back thousands of years. Many other breeds were developed more recently, some to work alongside us, helping with specific tasks, and others as designer and companion dogs bred for their looks and personality.

The inherited instinct to chase and herd is deeply rooted in the Border Collie.

INHERITED INSTINCTS

The majority of dogs no longer work, so why is it important to find out the reasons why they were originally developed? It all comes down to inheritance. Just as the domesticated dog has inherited instincts from the wolf, so the pet Border Collie has inherited, and retains, instincts from its working forebears. We might not need a Border Collie to work sheep, but the instinct to chase and herd is firmly rooted in the breed's make-up. It is only by finding out about inherited instincts that we get to know each

breed, and the behaviour and temperament that we are likely to see. This helps us to understand our dogs, and will also help in training if we want to curb or inhibit instincts that could cause problems in the modern world.

PUREBRED DOGS

The world of purebred dogs is divided into seven different groups in which breeds of similar type and origin are classified together.

GUNDOGS

These dogs were developed as shooting companions to work closely with a handler, finding and retrieving game for the gun. This type of dog is intelligent, biddable, and has considerable strength and stamina. There are different types of gundog, which specialise in different roles:

RETRIEVERS

In this group we find some of Britain's most popular dogs, such as the Labrador Retriever and the Golden Retriever, as well as the

Golden Retriever: Gentle, even-tempered and biddable.

*Labrador Retriever:
Currently the most
popular breed in the UK.*

*English Springer Spaniel: An
energetic companion with a
faithful, happy disposition.*

*Cocker Spaniel: A merry
dog that is quick to learn.*

lesser known Curly Coated Retriever and the Flat Coated Retriever. As working gundogs they excel in retrieving game from land and from the water. They also have an excellent sense of smell, which helps them to locate fallen game. Retrievers are generally friendly and outgoing, and breeds such as the Labrador Retriever and the Golden Retriever are the chosen breeds for assistance dogs. They enjoy the challenge of training, and as family companions they are second to none.

SPANIELS

This group includes the highly popular English Springer Spaniel and the Cocker Spaniel. Other spaniel breeds include the Welsh Springer, the Clumber, and the Sussex Spaniel. The spaniel's job was to track game and then to 'spring' it or flush it out from the undergrowth. Characteristically, you will see a spaniel out on a walk with his nose to the ground, tail wagging non-stop, investigating every scent he comes across. The spaniel has a merry temperament, and is a loving member of the family circle. If you can focus his attention, he has a brain to use, and will enjoy training exercises.

SETTERS AND POINTERS

Setters and Pointers were used to set and point game, holding it ready for the guns. Setters are the glamour dogs of the gundog group, including Irish, English and Red and White Setters. They are exuberant, fast-moving, fast-thinking dogs, and need some measure of control. The Pointer is a distinguished, athletic-looking dog that is known for his sweet nature. He can be very focused when working.

HUNT, POINT, RETRIEVE

These dogs were developed in Europe as all-purpose gundogs that could hunt, point and retrieve. The breeds in this group are becoming increasingly popular in the UK and include the Weimaraner, the German Shorthalred Pointer and the Hungarian Vizsla. These dogs are highly intelligent and like to work on their own initiative. They thrive on human companionship but do require firm handling.

HOUNDS

This group is divided into sighthounds and scenthounds.

SIGHTHOUNDS

As their names denotes, these are the hounds that hunt by sight. They include the true canine athletes, such as the Greyhound, the Saluki and the Borzoi. The Irish Wolfhound, the tallest of all breeds, is also in this group. These are elegant, fine-limbed dogs that can reach incredible speeds over short distances. They are loving, affectionate dogs, who enjoy their creature comforts. They make excellent companions, but they have a very strong instinct to chase. They will reach an acceptable level of obedience, but care needs to be taken to control the chasing instinct.

Weimaraner: An all-rounder with a high degree of intelligence.

Irish Setter: A happy-go-lucky type who needs to be controlled.

Greyhound: The ultimate canine athlete with a strong desire to chase.

Dachshund: The low-slung Dachshund may not look daring, but is reckoned to be bold to the point of rashness.

West Highland White Terrier: A spirited dog with an independent streak.

Staffordshire Bull Terrier: A dog that loves to clown around, but is fiercely courageous when required.

SCENTHOUNDS

All dogs have an excellent sense of smell, but scenthounds are in a different league. The dogs in this group include legendary tracking dogs, such as the Bloodhound and the Beagle, as well as the Dachshund, which was bred to burrow underground in search of rabbit, fox and badger. These breeds are diverse – but they are all governed by their love of investigating scents. This should be borne in mind, particularly when training a Recall!

TERRIERS

The British have a particular love of terriers, and many of the breeds in this group were developed in the UK. The majority of terrier breeds were developed to go to ground after fox and badger, and also to keep down vermin, such as rats and mice. These breeds, which include the popular Jack Russell and the West Highland White Terrier, are tough, rugged and courageous. They are highly intelligent, fun-loving companions and can achieve high standards in training if they are motivated.

This group also includes the Staffordshire Bull Terrier and the Bull Terrier, which both have a large and enthusiastic following. These breeds were originally developed as fighting dogs, and although this is now a distant part of their history, the instinct to fight remains a significant factor. With good training and socialisation, the instinct can be greatly diluted, and both the

Stafford and the Bully make excellent family companions. They are affectionate, outgoing and show a particular affinity with children. However, great care should be taken with these breeds when interacting with other dogs.

WORKING

This group includes the heavyweights of the dog world – the big, impressive-looking dogs that were used as guards. The Mastiff is one of the most ancient of all breeds; they were used by the Romans as dogs of war some 2,000 years before becoming formidable guard dogs. The Dogue de Bordeaux, the Neapolitan Mastiff and the Bullmastiff are all developed from the original Mastiff. These breeds are generally laidback and loving within their family circle but can be easily roused and need experienced handling.

The Boxer, the Dobermann and the Rottweiler are popular breeds in this group. They retain strong guarding instincts, and this needs to be channelled constructively. These dogs benefit from plenty of mental stimulation.

If you want a big, cuddly dog, there is the St Bernard, who specialised in search and rescue, and the Newfoundland, who is known as the fisherman's dog because of his work hauling in fishing nets in the freezing water of Newfoundland. Both these breeds are amiable and easygoing, and will achieve a reasonable level of obedience.

Rottweiler: This breed tends to attract adverse publicity, but in the right hands, a Rottweiler can reach high levels of obedience.

Siberian Husky: A people-orientated dog that makes friends easily, but needs plenty of occupation.

Dogue de Bordeaux: With experienced handling, this breed makes an outstanding companion.

21

Border Collie: The workaholic of the canine world will excel in all the competitive sports.

German Shepherd Dog: The exceptional qualities of the German Shepherd are perfectly suited to police work.

The Alaskan Malamute and the Siberian Husky were developed to work in extreme conditions, pulling sleds over ice and snow from dawn to dusk. These are high-energy breeds and should not be considered unless you can provide sufficient exercise and stimulation.

PASTORAL

These are the breeds that are associated with working with livestock. They include the Border Collie, the German Shepherd Dog, and the Old English Sheepdog. Some of the pastoral breeds, such as the Rough Collie, have not been used as working sheepdogs for many generations, and their instincts have become very diluted. However, the Border Collie still has a tremendous work ethic and can easily become obsessed with chasing, or with herding substitute objects such as footballs, if he is not given an outlet to his mental capabilities. However, if you want a dog to compete with in one of the canine disciplines, such as obedience or agility, this is the breed for you.

The German Shepherd Dog was originally developed as a herding dog, but it was not long before security forces recognised the breed's courage, loyalty and intelligence, and it has become the police dog of choice all over the world. This is a dog that is fiercely loyal towards his family and thrives on a high level of training.

The larger members of this group, such as the Pyrenean Mountain Dog and the Maremma Sheepdog, were used to guard the flock, and they both have strong protective instincts.

TOY

The Toy breeds are the ultimate companion dogs. Most were developed purely as lap dogs that could be pampered by the nobility. The King Charles and the Cavalier King Charles Spaniel were royal favourites, and thc Pckingese was treasured by the Imperial Court in China. There are some breeds, such as the Yorkshire Terrier, that have a less noble background. This breed was developed as a ratter, and was highly skilled at putting down vermin in the homes of the poor coalmining families in Yorkshire.

The attraction of Toy dogs is the fact that they are small and need very little exercise. But these breeds are not small in personality. The tiny Chihuahua, for example, is an alert watch dog, and is ready to take on all-comers. The Yorkshire Terrier is bold and feisty and very much a terrier at heart. These breeds tend to be quick-witted and intelligent, and are capable of being trained to a high standard.

UTILITY

This group is hugely diverse, ranging from the Dalmatian to the Shih Tzu. In reality, it is the group for breeds that were originally bred for a purpose, but this no longer exists. The Dalmatian, for example,

Cavalier King Charles Spaniel: One of the most biddable of the Toy breeds.

Yorkshire Terrier: Small in size, but big in personality.

Dalmatian: This is an outgoing breed that needs firm handling during adolescence.

Poodle: This is the Standard Poodle, the largest of the three varieties.

Labradoodle: A cross between a Labrador Retriever and a Poodle.

was bred to run alongside horse-drawn carriages. The Tibetan breeds, such as the Lhasa Apso, the Shih Tzu and the Tibetan Spaniel, were temple watch dogs, and the Shar Pei has been used as a hunter, a herder, a guard and a fighting dog. The popular Poodle, which comes in three sizes – Standard, Miniature and Toy – is in this group, as well as Britain's national breed, the Bulldog.

The breeds in this group are so different; it is a matter of doing your homework and finding out what are the over-riding traits in each individual breed.

CROSSBREEDS

This term is used when two different purebred dogs are bred from, producing offspring that are a combination of both breeds. For example, the Guide Dogs for the Blind Association regularly breed Labrador Retrievers with Golden Retrievers, as this gives the ideal combination of calmness, steadiness and intelligence that is required for guiding work. There are a number of other combinations that are becoming increasingly popular among pet owners, such as the Labradoodle – a cross between a Labrador Retriever and a Poodle. There is a degree of risk associated with crossbreeds, as the blend of the two breeds, both in terms of appearance and temperament, can be variable. However, when two breeds share a similar physical type and mental make-up, such as

Heinz 57: You never know how a mongrel is going to turn out – but they often make great family dogs.

the Labrador Retriever and the Golden Retriever, it can produce excellent working and companion dogs.

MIXED BREEDS

This is the term that is often used for a mongrel, which is a dog of no known parentage, sometimes also called a 'Heinz 57'. Its parents may themselves be crossbreeds or mongrels, so it is impossible to guess what has gone into the mix. The problem with a mixed breed is that you have no idea of what you are going to get in terms of size, shape, coat type or temperament until the dog is fully grown. However, there are many pet owners who have had mongrels, and claim they are the best dogs in the world. They often suffer from fewer health problems than purebred dogs.

TOOLS OF THE TRADE

Chapter 3

Communication is the key to good dog training, and before we take on the role of teacher and leader, we need to open up pathways so both dog and handler can tune into each other. We have looked at the ways in which dogs communicate with each other, now we need to work out how dogs can pick up the signals that we give.

OUR BODY LANGUAGE

Dogs are very sensitive to body language and will understand our intentions by our actions. Many owners report that their dogs can sense their moods, and will react differently if they are happy, sad or short tempered.

If we are to use body language as an effective means of

communication, we need to become more aware of how we appear to our dogs.

- If you get down to your dog's level, he is likely to see you as an equal rather than as a leader. Obviously, it is fine to have a play or a cuddle with your dog at his level, but make sure it is on your terms and do not allow the dog to become too boisterous.
- If you stand upright, your dog is more likely to respect you. However, if a dog is worried or nervous, you would want to appear less daunting, and you would go down to your dog's level.
- A dog is strongly motivated by movement, and he will be quick to respond to your actions. This can work well when you are training. For example, you can encourage your dog to respond to the Recall by opening your arms wide and welcoming him. Conversely, you can train the "Wait" or "Stay" by using a hand signal – palm held flat towards the dog – which effectively blocks his movement.

BEWARE!

Children move quickly and unpredictably, and it is important to understand how a dog will interpret this. For example, if a child runs away, waving their arms in the air, we will understand that the child is frightened and trying to get away. However, a dog will be stimulated

It is great to give your dog a cuddle, but bear in mind that when you are at his level, he will view you as a playmate.

You will show more authority if you stand upright. This is important with breeds such as the Dogue de Bordeaux, which may seek to challenge your status.

Play between children and dogs should always be supervised.

If you are teaching your dog to "Stay", you should avoid eye contact.

by the movement, which will probably be accompanied by high-pitched shouts. He will want to give chase, and will try to jump up to reach the waving arms. This is why all interactions between dogs and young children should be closely supervised. A dog that knocks over a small child who is running away will very rarely have bad intentions; he is simply reading the body language he sees, and interpreting it as an invitation to chase. It is therefore vitally important that children and dogs learn how to behave in each other's company (see pages 49-51).

SEEING EYE TO EYE

- Dogs do not read our facial expressions, but they are very aware of eye contact. If you give eye contact to your dog, he will see it as a very direct form of communication. For example, if you want your dog to "Stay", and you walk away a few paces, you must avoid eye contact with him, otherwise he will think you are signalling to him, and he will probably get up and follow you.
- In a different context, a dog may see eye contact as a challenge. For example, if a dog has climbed up on the sofa and is trying to elevate his status, he will see eye contact from you as a direct challenge, and his behaviour may escalate. In this situation, it is better to avoid eye contact and distract his attention by giving him a positive cue, such as "Come", or even

A highly trained dog may build up an extensive repertoire of cues that he responds to.

showing him a toy and inviting him to play with it. This avoids confrontation; you will be back in control of the situation, and it has a positive outcome.

TALKING TO DOGS

We rely so completely on language, we can find it hard to communicate with animals that view vocal sounds on a different, and far less significant, level than we do. However, a well-trained dog can build up a surprisingly large repertoire of commands or cues that he responds to. How many times have you heard an owner talk about their dog, saying: "He understands every word I say". In fact, the dog does not understand language in the way we understand each other, he has learnt to associate the sound of a word with

the appropriate action. For example, when you train your dog to "Sit", you will lure him into position with a treat. When he reacts to the lure and sits, you add the cue "Sit". The dog will quickly associate the word with the action he is rewarded for, and will sit on cue.

TONE OF VOICE

A dog will pick up a number of cues that he responds to, but he will be far more sensitive to your tone of voice. He will be quick to learn that a warm, encouraging, positive tone of voice means he has earned your approval, and he will be motivated to continue with the behaviour he is showing. Equally, he will learn that a deep, gruff voice means that you are displeased and are calling a halt to his behaviour.

REWARDING YOUR DOG

When you are training your dog, you will want to use all the tools that are available so you can develop and enrich your relationship. We have seen that a dog learns more quickly and more effectively when we use positive, reward-based training methods. We must therefore find out what a dog values as a reward so that we can provide motivation, encouragement, and, at times, reassurance.

Rewards can be divided into different categories:

STROKING

The dog is a tactile animal and enjoys the sensation of being stroked and cuddled. A mother will lick her puppies to clean them, but also to soothe them. In the wild, adult wolves will groom each other

Stroking cements the bond between dog and owner, and also rewards the dog for good behaviour.

as a way of keeping their coats clean, but also to cement the bond between them.

Pros
• Physical praise is pleasurable for the dog, and you don't have to go out and buy it!

Cons
• You cannot use food treats at a distance.

VERBAL PRAISE

You can tell your dog he is a "Good boy" or a "Clever boy" and he will bask in your approval. From the first moment of contact with people, a puppy will relate to a warm, happy, encouraging tone of voice, as he associates this with good things, such as physical praise or being called at mealtimes.

Most dogs see food treats as a big reward.

Pros
• Your voice is readily available, and as we are mainly verbal communicators, most people find it is a natural and effective training tool.

Cons
• We sometimes speak in monotones, and fail to use varying tones to make ourselves sound exciting and motivating. A dog will tune out of his handler's voice, seeing it as pleasant background noise rather than something he should respond to.

FOOD TREATS

In the majority of cases, the way to a dog's heart is through his stomach. A dog learns to respect you because you provide his daily food, so when you give extra treats he will love and respect you even more.

Pros
• A dog will quickly learn that he has to work for his treats, and this will make him a willing pupil.
• You can vary the treats you use from low-grade, such as dried food, to high-value rewards, such as cheese, liver or sausage. This means you can vary your reward and introduce tasty treats if you are teaching a new exercise, or if your dog has responded to a long-distance Recall when you are in the park.

Cons
• It can be tricky to reward your dog with a food treat at the exact moment he has responded correctly, which can lead to

TOP TIP

If you are using food treats, make sure you deduct the quantity of food given in training from your dog's daily ration.

mixed messages.

- A greedy dog may try to mug his owner to get at the treats, so you must introduce discipline when you are using food rewards.
- Obesity is a major problem in the dog population, and if you give too many food treats, your dog will pile on the pounds.

A game with a toy is a fun way of interacting with your dog.

PLAY

Some dogs love to play, and a game with a toy is considered to be a top reward. When you are using a toy as a reward, make sure you reserve a favourite toy for training sessions, ensuring your dog cannot get access to it at other times. This means that the training toy will have added value, as it is not freely available.

Pros

- A game with a toy means interaction between dog and handler. You are providing fun, so you are the focus of attention. Equally, you are in control of the toy, which enhances your leadership status.
- A dog that is toy mad will learn to work for his toy, knowing the reward will come when the exercise is completed to your satisfaction.

Cons

- You need to plan training sessions with some precision, as you will need to break off for a game at regular intervals.
- Some dogs get too boisterous when toys are introduced, so you need to retain some measure of control.

Spend quality time with your dog and he will thrive on the attention you give him.

COMBINING REWARDS

When you are training your dog, you will probably find that you use a combination of rewards, such as verbal praise followed by a game, a food treat or a stroke. Mix and match works well for everyone, so vary the rewards so that your dog remains focused and motivated.

GIVING YOUR ATTENTION

There is one other way of interacting with your dog, which is perhaps the most effective of all training tools. A dog that understands his place in the family pack will enjoy getting attention from all the family, but he will particularly value attention from the person he sees as his leader. Spend quality time with your dog, stroking him, playing with him, or providing food treats when he has

A dog needs to learn 'appropriate' behaviour.

co-operated with you. Your dog will see attention from you as the biggest reward he can get, and this provides a sure foundation to all future training.

CHASTISING YOUR DOG

The aim of every trainer is to have a happy, well-behaved dog that responds to commands and never gets up to mischief. However, we have to remember that dogs are animals, not machines. There are times when your dog finds temptation hard to resist and, in your eyes, he commits a crime.

It may be that you have left some food out at a level he can reach and he has been quick to take advantage, or he may have ignored a Recall command because he has met a new canine friend in the park, and he would rather play than come back to you. In both scenarios, the dog is behaving naturally. All dogs are natural scavengers; he does not see stealing the roast chicken as a criminal act – he is merely making the most of what providence has put in his way. Similarly, the dog is naturally a sociable animal, and meeting and playing with one of his own kind is likely to be more rewarding for him than coming back you.

How do you show your dog that you disapprove of his behaviour, and, more importantly, how do you correct it?

PHYSICAL PUNISHMENT

The old-fashioned school of dog

training believed that it did no harm to chastise a dog by smacking him or by jerking him back to order on a choke chain. Fortunately, dog trainers have made considerable advances, and it is now widely understood that physical punishment or harsh handling has no part in training dogs, or, indeed, in any aspect of our relationship with dogs.

Pros

- There are none, except that you have frightened your dog into stopping his undesirable behaviour. However, there is no guarantee that he has learnt from the experience.

Cons

- Physical violence against any animal is mindless and highly objectionable.
- A dog that is forced to learn through negative experiences will be cowed and fearful, and will not be motivated to work for you. If he co-operates, it is only because he is frightened of the bad consequences that might result if he steps out of line.
- A dog that is exposed to physical punishment may become brooding and resentful, and may even strike back if he is being victimised.

Verbal punishment

It is tempting to think that if you tell off a dog for some wrongdoing, he will understand why you are displeased. However, dogs do not come equipped with a moral conscience and will not understand why you think that raiding the bin is a bad idea.

If you catch your dog 'red-handed' you can use your voice to call an instant halt to his behaviour.

You can use a gruff, growling tone of voice to convey your displeasure.

Jumping up is a way of demanding attention.

Ignoring your dog will make him realise that the behaviour he is offering is not working for him.

In this instance, you can use your voice to call a halt to his actions and to show that you are displeased.

As with verbal praise, your dog does not understand what you are saying, he is picking up on your tone of voice. A deep, gruff, stern tone contrasts sharply with the warm, happy tone of voice he enjoys hearing when he is being rewarded. In the same way as a mother would tell off her puppy by giving a warning growl, you can convey your displeasure by using a low, growly tone of voice.

Pros
- Your dog will respond to the strong, disapproving tone of your voice and he will know he has displeased his owner.
- You can use your voice as a shock tactic, surprising your dog in the midst of his crime with a stern command of "No", which will often be enough to halt him in his tracks.

Cons
- You need to develop an authoritative tone of voice, or your dog will not believe that you must be respected.

IGNORING YOUR DOG
A dog will work hard to win your attention, and sometimes this can lead to undesirable attention-seeking behaviour, such as jumping up, whining or barking. The most effective way of correcting this is to deny your dog the attention he is demanding until he changes his behaviour.

For example, if you have a dog that repeatedly jumps up at you, turn your back on him and ignore him. It will not take long before the dog realises that jumping up is producing no response from you,

You need to find out what is the best reward for your dog so that he is willing to co-operate with

and he will try a different behaviour. The skill of the trainer is to wait until the dog has made a 'good' decision, i.e. standing with all four feet on the ground, and then to reward him by giving him the attention he seeks.

Just as giving attention to your dog is highly rewarding, and therefore effective as a training tool, the opposite reaction of ignoring your dog is equally powerful. See page 146.

GET YOUR TIMING RIGHT

When you reward your dog and, equally, when you reprimand him, you need to get your timing right. It is vitally important to react within one or two seconds when you give praise or correction otherwise the dog will not associate his behaviour with your response.

When your dog performs an exercise correctly, be quick to praise and he will rapidly learn that this is the behaviour you want. (See Clicker Training, page 90).

It is much harder to get your timing right when you need to correct your dog. It is almost impossible not to shout at your dog when you discover he has chewed your slippers, but unless you catch him red-handed, he will have no idea why you are angry with him. He will associate the behaviour he has offered in the last couple of seconds – maybe greeting you as you walk through the door – as the cause of your anger.

Do not be fooled into thinking that your dog understands his 'crime' because he looks guilty. He is simply reacting to your disapproval.

PUTTING IT INTO PRACTICE

Understanding the general principles of how and why dogs behave the way they do, and how we can best communicate with them is a crucial part of training. But it is important to bear in mind that every dog is an individual. Your dog is special: and you need to find out his likes and dislikes, what motivates him, and what makes him anxious, so that you can tailor your training methods and get the very best out of him.

EARLY LEARNING

Chapter 4

One of the most common mistakes among new dog owners is to delay the start of training. A new puppy has so much to get used to, it may seem harsh to start introducing rules and regulations from day one. If you are taking on an older rescued dog, you may feel tempted to pamper him for the first few weeks to help him get over the trauma of moving homes. However, the old adage "start as you mean to go on", is never truer than when it is applied to dog training. This does not mean you are going to lay down the law like a dictator from the moment your dog steps over the threshold. But the best way of settling a new puppy, or an older dog, is to introduce him to your ways, with kindness and with firmness, so that he finds his place in the family circle. A dog's principle desire is to feel safe and secure, and this can only happen if he knows his boundaries and respects the leadership that is being presented to him.

ARRIVING HOME

The day you collect a puppy or an older dog is exciting for you, but it is daunting for the newcomer. Everything familiar is left behind, and, in the case of a puppy, it is the first time of coping alone, without his mother or littermates. Do not get carried away and invite all your friends and neighbours round to inspect the new arrival, but, instead, concentrate on making the transition from one home to another as calm and stress-free as possible. An older, rescued dog will find his feet more quickly, as he will generally be used to living in a home and interacting with different people. However, it is worth following the procedure outlined below, making adaptations where necessary, in order to help him to settle.

- To begin with, take your puppy into the garden and give him a chance to explore. Talk to him in a warm, friendly tone of voice to give him reassurance. Call him to you and then give him lots of praise. This is step one in teaching the Recall (see page 123).
- If your puppy toilets, so much the better. This will give you the opportunity to praise him, marking the start of the housetraining process (see page 61).

Arriving in a new home is a daunting experience for a puppy.

Give your puppy a chance to explore his new surroundings.

- Take your puppy into the kitchen/utility room and show him his sleeping quarters. Ideally you will have bought a crate, and you can take a few minutes to introduce him to it. For information on Crate Training, see page 55.
- Allow your pup to explore the rooms where he is allowed access. He needs to find out which parts of the house he is free to use, and which are the no-go areas. If you want to prevent your puppy going into specific rooms, or stop him going upstairs, a stair-gate is a very useful purchase.
- Hopefully, you will have prepared your house and garden to withstand an inquisitive exploring puppy. If your pup tries to get hold of something that he is not allowed, such as the bottom of the curtains, tell him "No" in a firm voice, and offer him a toy that he is allowed to play with.
- To begin with he will probably be too small to jump up on the furniture, but the first time he tries to do this, tell him "No" and distract him with a toy or a treat. It is vital that your pup understands his place in the home right from the start.

INTRODUCING THE FAMILY

If you have children, you will need to supervise interactions with the puppy. If you have older children, you can teach them how to play sensibly with the pup, but small children should always be supervised. A game can get out of hand in a matter of seconds, and the consequences could be disastrous. Adopt the following procedure when introducing your puppy to the family:

- Get the children to sit on the floor. A puppy can be very wriggly, and you do not want to risk the pup being dropped from a height.
- Give each of the children a treat, and let the puppy meet each child in turn and take the treat. Encourage the children to stroke the pup calmly and gently.
- You can introduce a toy, such as a ragger, and let the pup tug the end of it. Make sure the game does not get too boisterous, as you want everyone to remain calm and quiet. High-pitched voices will stimulate the puppy and he will become over-excited.
- When the children are on their feet, make sure they do not run or wave their arms about when the puppy is with them. This will encourage the pup to jump up and chase them, which will inevitably end in tears.

Try to keep the situation as calm as possible when you introduce your puppy to the family.

Play biting is natural behaviour between littermates.

PLAY BITING

If the puppy attempts to nip fingers as he takes a treat, or as the children stroke him, you must put a stop to it at once. The puppy may only be playing – in fact, he is behaving in the same way as he would when interacting with his littermates – but it can be very painful. Try the following strategy:

- Get a treat in your hand and show your puppy what you have. Make sure he does not snatch from you.
- Close your fist on the treat, and hold your fist out towards the puppy.
- Let him sniff your hand, and, when he is calm, preferably when he is sitting, open your fist so the pup can take the treat from the palm of your hand.
- Repeat this several times. If the puppy tries to scrabble or bite at your fist, say "No", and withdraw

If play biting is not curbed in puppyhood, it can become a major problem when a dog has his adult teeth.

39

Allow the puppy and adult dog to get to know each other on neutral territory.

your hand. Try again in a few seconds, waiting until the pup is calm before you present the treat. In time, the puppy will learn that he is only rewarded with the treat when he does not snatch.

- When the puppy is taking the treat calmly every time you present it, introduce a verbal cue, such as "Gently". With practice, the pup will associate the cue with what he is doing, and will understand that he must inhibit his behaviour and co-operate with you.

When your puppy has learnt the verbal cue "Gently" you can apply it in different situations, such as if he is getting too boisterous when playing with toys, or if he attempts to nip when he is being cuddled.

INTRODUCING OTHER ANIMALS

If you already have pets at home, you will need to introduce the puppy to his new housemates. Again, the watchword is to keep interactions calm and stress-free so that relations get off on a good footing.

THE RESIDENT DOG

If you have a resident dog, it is best to introduce the puppy in the garden. This allows everyone more space, and the resident dog will not feel as though his territory is being invaded.

- Start off with the resident dog on the lead, and allow him to sniff the puppy. The adult will quickly realise that he is dealing with a baby and will understand that the pup is no threat.

- If your adult dog is too rough in his greeting, call him back to you so he focuses his attention on you, and then praise him, maybe giving him a treat. Let the lead go loose and allow him to greet the puppy again. Praise him lavishly if he interacts calmly.

- If you are happy with the way the situation is progressing, let your dog off the lead, and allow him to meet and greet the puppy independently. Again, if he is too rough, call him back to you and give him a treat. It is important that the older dog keeps interacting with you and realises that you are in charge of the situation.

After the initial introduction, take a step back and allow the two dogs to get to know each other without

Ideally, a cat will stand his ground, and this will inhibit a puppy's instinct to chase.

interference from you. Dogs speak their own language, and they need to establish their relationship with each other. You are the leader, but they need to work out where they stand in relation to each other. Obviously, the older dog will have the elevated status to begin with, and that is why you should never tell him off for an occasional growl at the puppy. In effect, he is teaching the puppy where his boundaries lie, and this is a valuable lesson for the puppy.

Initially, you will need to supervise all interactions between the adult and the puppy until you are confident that they have reached an understanding. If you are going out, or are leaving the dogs overnight, make sure they are separated just in case trouble erupts. Ideally, the puppy will be in a crate where he will safe and secure.

In time, when the puppy matures, the hierarchy may change, and the youngster may assume top-dog status. Do not try to interfere or attempt to change the course of events. The two dogs will come to a mutual, harmonious agreement far more quickly if you are not part of the equation.

FRIEND OR FOE?
Dogs and cats are traditionally portrayed as enemies, but this does not have to be the case. The best friendships are formed when a puppy and kitten grow up together, but if initial interactions between a cat and a puppy are supervised, they should achieve a mutual understanding.

- For the first few meetings, put your cat in a carrier so the puppy can sniff him and get acquainted, but he cannot pounce or chase. The cat is safe from danger, and equally, the puppy is safe because the cat cannot swipe at him with his sharp claws.
- If your puppy gets over-excited and tries to scrabble at the carrier, distract his attention by calling him and giving him a treat. Practise this a few times, and then introduce the verbal cue "Leave". Say this in a firm tone of voice, and, as soon as your puppy responds, lighten your tone and call him to you. You can then praise him and give him a treat.
- The next step is to introduce the

two animals when the cat is out of his carrier. Before you do this, make sure there is a high surface that he can escape to if necessary. Adopt exactly the same procedure as when the cat was in his carrier, distracting your puppy when he gets too focused on the cat, and then rewarding him. In time, he will learn that it is more rewarding to respond to you.

Inevitably, there will be a moment when your pup attempts to chase, and, in most cases, the cat is very quick to get out of the way. If he hisses or spits at the puppy from his elevated position, this will help to teach the pup that the cat must be respected. It takes time for harmonious relations to be established, but neither animal will come to any harm if you supervise all interactions.

PETS IN CAGES

If your pup is coming into a multi-pet household, with small pets, such as a hamster or a guinea pig or a budgerigar in a cage, he needs to learn that they are strictly out of bounds.

- Allow your puppy to come near to the cage, but make sure you have him firmly under control, so he cannot frighten the inmate. Let the puppy look, but do not let him get close to the cage.
- The puppy will be fascinated by the tiny creature, so your job is to divert his attention so that he

Some dogs will learn to live peacefully alongside small, furry animals – but it is never worth taking risks.

focuses on you. Again, use his name and when he switches his attention from the cage, give him lots of praise and reward him with a treat.
- Next, give the verbal cue "Leave", making sure you sound stern, and reward your puppy the instant he responds.
- Practise this frequently so that the novelty of the small creature in the cage wears off.

If you follow this procedure, you should be able to control your puppy, but do not make the mistake of trusting him. Small pets and dogs are not a good mix, and some dogs, with a strong chasing instinct, will

not be able to resist temptation. Small pets should be housed well out of reach, and your puppy should never be allowed in the same room without supervision. If you are keeping small pets outside, such as rabbits or guinea pigs in a hutch, the same rules apply. The hutch must be 100 per cent secure, and should be located in a part of the garden that your puppy cannot access.

CRATE TRAINING

This is one of the most important lessons you need to teach your puppy when he arrives in his new home. A crate, used correctly, is a great aid to rearing puppies, and guarantees that your puppy will be safe at times when you cannot supervise him. The crate you buy should be big enough to accommodate your dog comfortably when he is an adult.

PREPARING THE CRATE

- Line the floor of the crate with bedding. The best type to buy is synthetic fleece, which does not hold moisture. It is machine-washable and easy to dry.
- If you have a young puppy who is not going to be able to go through the night without spending, place newspaper in the front section of the crate. This means your pup can spend without soiling his bedding.
- Ideally, the crate should be located in a quiet part of the

house, such as the utility room or a hallway, so your puppy can get some peace from the hurly burly of the household. However, make sure the crate is placed out of draughts and in a place that does not get too warm in the summer or too cold in the winter.

INTRODUCING THE CRATE

Many breeders use a playpen as the puppies they are rearing get bigger, and if this is the case, you will have a head start, as your pup will understand the concept of settling in a confined area. If you introduce the crate in a positive way, your pup will soon see it as a safe haven where he can rest undisturbed.

- Open the door of the crate and kneel down beside it. Call your puppy to you, and show him that you have a treat.
- Throw the treat into the crate and your puppy will follow it in. Give him lots of praise and give him another treat while he is in the crate. Repeat this several times so that the puppy thinks that going in and out of the crate is a game.
- When it is time to feed your puppy, place the bowl inside the crate and close the door. Your puppy will be so busy eating, he will scarcely notice. The aim is to build up a good association with the crate so that your puppy wants to go in it.
- You can build up the length of time that your pup spends in the crate. It will help if you leave a toy, such as a rubber Kong filled

A puppy will soon learn to settle in his crate.

with food, in the crate, as this will give your puppy an occupation so that he will not mind being confined.

Do's...

- Use the crate when you have to go out, or when you cannot supervise the puppy properly. In this way, you know he will be safe and cannot get up to mischief.
- Make the crate even more den-like by draping a blanket over the sides of the crate.

...and don't's

- Do not use the crate for lengthy periods, except when you are confining your puppy overnight.
- Do not allow your puppy to wear his collar when he is in the crate in case it catches on the wire, which could result in a nasty accident.
- Do not allow children to disturb the puppy when he is in his crate.
- Never use the crate as a means of punishing your puppy.

TOP TIPS

When you see a litter of puppies sleeping, they all lie in a pile, enjoying the warmth of each other's bodies. You can replicate this by putting a covered hot-water bottle in the bedding. Make sure you fill it with luke-warm water, and ensure the stopper is secure.

You can also try leaving the radio on at a low volume, which may provide comforting background noise.

To begin with, a puppy will miss the companionship of his littermates.

THE FIRST NIGHT

This is an occasion that new puppy owners dread – and it can become an ordeal if you let it. Obviously a puppy is going to be upset the first night in his new home. He will miss the companionship of his littermates, and he will not understand why his new 'people friends' have deserted him. However, if you establish a night-time regime, your pup will understand that this is what happens every night, and he will learn to settle in the full knowledge that he will see you the following morning.

Work at the following bedtime routine:

- Check the crate to make sure it is clean, with cosy bedding at the back, and newspaper at the front. You can leave a toy in the crate, as long as it is 100 per cent safe.
- Take your puppy out just before

going to bed so he has a chance to relieve himself.

- Open the crate door, and encourage him to go inside with a treat or a small biscuit.
- Shut the crate and leave the room immediately, without making a drama out o-f your departure.
- Inevitably, you will hear your puppy protesting, but you must deafen your ears to his cries. If you go to him, he will think that barking and whining has paid dividends – and he will try it every night. Remember, the puppy is safe in his crate; he simply needs to learn that he can cope on his own.

MEALTIMES

For the vast majority of dogs, mealtimes are the high spot of the day. It is also an important time for bonding between dog and owner, as the dog sees you as the provider, and will willingly give his respect.

You can use mealtimes as constructive training sessions, as you can be certain you have your puppy's undivided attention. As well using mealtimes to build up a good association with the crate, there are other lessons you can teach your puppy:

- When you are preparing the meal, make sure your puppy is calm and quiet. If he tries to jump up at you, or barks impatiently, suspend your preparations. Do not resume until your puppy is quiet. This teaches your dog good manners,

With practice, your puppy will learn to "Sit" and "Wait" before you put the bowl down.

and he is also learning that attention-seeking behaviour does not pay off.

- When the meal is ready, hold the bowl out of reach. Initially, the puppy may jump up but, as he looks up at the bowl, he will almost certainly go into the Sit. (For more information on teaching "Sit", see page 95).
- When your puppy gets a little

older, you can ask him to "Wait" a couple of seconds before you put the bowl down. (For more information on teaching your puppy to "Wait" see page 113.)

- When your puppy is eating, kneel down beside him and drop a little extra food into his bowl. This will teach him to welcome your presence rather than becoming possessive over his food bowl.

FADDY FEEDERS

When a puppy is settling into a new home, he may be reluctant to eat, or he may not eat all the food you put down for him. There are two principle reasons for this:

- The puppy is distracted by his new environment and he cannot settle to eat his food.
- The pup is used to the rivalry of feeding with his littermates, and he is not sufficiently motivated to eat.

In the vast majority of cases, a pup will take a few days to settle and will then eat everything you put in front of him. It is therefore inadvisable to try to tempt your puppy's appetite by adding tasty treats, or changing his diet because you are worried that the pup does not like his food. The result of doing this could be to give him an upset stomach, and to make him a picky feeder.

A pup will not take long to realise that if he holds out on you, he will get something better to eat – and you will be on a treadmill, trying to find ever more appetising food.

If your pup is reluctant to eat at first, simply take up his bowl after 10 minutes, and feed him fresh food at his next meal. Obviously, if your pup shows any signs of ill health, or continues to refuse food, you should contact your vet for advice.

BONES AND CHEWS

Puppies need to chew as their milk teeth fall out and their adult teeth come through. An adult dog will also benefit from having a bone or a chew, which will help to keep teeth clean and gums healthy. However, some dogs can become possessive over bones, so it is important that this behaviour is never allowed to develop.

- When you give a bone, make sure your puppy or adult dog is supervised. This prevents potential choking accidents, and it also means that your puppy cannot run off and 'guard' his bone.
- When your puppy has had his bone for a few minutes, go up to him and stroke him, so that he does not resent your presence.
- Offer him a treat and gently take the bone from him. A puppy should always be prepared to give up a bone on request. Praise him and then let him have the bone again.
- Repeat this a couple of times so your pup learns that he must give up his bone – but he will get it back.
- When the pup has had a good

Some puppies are picky about their food, but it is important not to become over-indulgent.

A bone is considered high value, so your dog must learn to give it up on request.

gnaw at his bone, you need to decide when the 'bone session' is at an end and take the bone from him. You can give him the bone on another occasion, but you should not allow your pup to think that he 'owns' the bone.

You may think this training regime is unnecessary with a small puppy, but it is vital that he learns how to behave with objects that he values.

HOUSE TRAINING

This aspect of training should start from the moment your puppy arrives in his new home, and you should put all your efforts into establishing a toilet routine over the first few weeks. The harder you work at house training, the sooner your puppy will learn what is required.

GOLDEN RULES

1 Set aside an area of the garden to be used for toileting. This teaches the puppy that he should spend when you take him out to his toileting spot, and it also makes cleaning up easier.

2 Choose a verbal cue, such as "Busy", and use it every time your dog spends. This will teach him to associate the word with the action, and he will learn to spend on command.

3 Take your puppy out at regular intervals:
   • When he wakes in the morning
   • After meals
   • After play sessions
   • Last thing at night
   • As a minimum requirement, your puppy will need to go out every two hours throughout the day – more if he has just had a hectic play session or has woken from a nap.

4 Accompany your puppy into the garden so you can give the verbal cue, and praise him when he performs.

5 When your pup has performed, have a little play with him so that he does not think that the fun of being outside stops as soon as he has spent. If he is taken back to the house immediately, he may start to adopt delaying tactics.

6 Read your puppy's body language, and he will tell you when he needs to spend. Most pups come to an abrupt halt, sniff, and circle before performing. If you see the signs, you can react in time.

AT NIGHT

You cannot expect a young puppy to be clean overnight to begin with, but if you use a crate, it will certainly hasten the process. A puppy hates to soil his sleeping quarters and so he has an in-built desire to keep his crate clean.

In the early stages, he can spend on newspaper at the front of the crate, so he does not have to soil his bedding, but as soon as he is physically able to go through the night, he will wait until he is released before spending.

Make sure your puppy's last feed is no later than 6pm, and restrict his access to water after 8pm. In this way, you are giving your puppy every chance of being clean overnight.

COMMON MISTAKES

If house training is not going according to plan, you are the one to blame. You may think you are following the rules, but if the message is not getting through, you need to review the situation.

Here are some of the mistakes that are most commonly made:

- You are not letting your puppy out often enough. You may seem to be continually taking your puppy out, but unless you stick to the guidelines – taking your pup out even more frequently when you think he needs to go – the pup is bound to have accidents in the house.
- You are not accompanying your pup into the garden for toileting. It may be cold or raining, but you need to go out with him every time so that he learns what is required, and is praised when he performs.

- You are letting him stray outside his toileting area so he thinks he is free to explore rather than concentrating on what you want him to do.
- You have tried to cut corners by taking your pup back to the house as soon as he has performed rather than having a short play session with him. The pup reacts by delaying his toileting to prolong his time in the garden. Inevitably, you get fed up waiting, so you take him back inside before he has spent.
- You are not supervising your puppy in the house. If a pup is

Take your puppy out at regular intervals and he will soon learn what is required.

left alone in a room, he may find a discreet spot and spend. This can easily become a habit, and is exacerbated if the carpet is not thoroughly cleaned. The puppy starts to think that his toileting area is in the place in the house that he has chosen.

WHEN ACCIDENTS HAPPEN
Despite all your best efforts, your puppy will have the occasional 'accident' in the house before his toileting routine is fully established. What should you do?

The old-fashioned remedy was to reprimand the puppy and rub his nose in the mess. Fortunately, our understanding of dogs has advanced and that treatment is not only considered harsh but completely ineffectual. Unless you catch your puppy 'in the act' he will not connect your response with what he has done, and he will learn nothing from the experience.

If you discover an accident in the house, simply clean it up, and remind yourself to be more vigilant in future. Make sure you use a deodoriser on the carpet to eliminate all traces of smell, otherwise your puppy might be tempted to use that spot again.

If you catch your puppy red-handed, you can turn the mistake into a lesson. Quickly, pick up the puppy and take him outside to his toileting area. Give your verbal cue, and hopefully, he will oblige.

Do not allow your puppy to roam the house without supervision, as he may find his own toileting area.

When he does, remember to give lots of praise – at least your puppy got it right in the end!

HANDLING
It is important that your puppy gets used to being handled so that you can care for him in all situations. This is important for routine grooming, and also if he needs to be checked over by a vet. If a pup is used to being handled, he will accept the procedure without resentment. This is important with all puppies, but it is especially important if you have chosen a longcoated breed, such as a Shih Tzu, which is going to need extensive grooming when the adult coat comes through.

Accustom your puppy to handling

by practising the following regime:
- Place your puppy on a flat, non-slip surface. If you are using a table, you can cover it with a piece of vet bed or a rubber mat. Make sure you have some small, bite-size treats at the ready.
- Start by stroking your puppy from head to tail. If he tries to wriggle or mouth you, say "No" in a firm voice, and as soon as he quietens and co-operates, give him a treat.
- With a soft brush, gently groom the coat. Talk reassuringly to your puppy, telling him what a "good boy" he is.
- Pick up each paw in turn and check the pads and the nails. Reward your puppy when he is standing calmly.
- Check the ears. They should be clean and free from odour.
- Part the lips and check the teeth and gums. Your pup may struggle when you try to do this, so be firm but reassuring. It is important that you complete the task or your pup will think he can take evasive action and you will stop pestering him.

After a few sessions, your pup will learn to settle on the table, and will enjoy the quality time he is spending with you. This is an invaluable lesson, as a pup who is used to all-over handling at an early age will accept grooming, teeth cleaning, nail trimming and all other health procedures that are required without making a fuss.

HANDLING

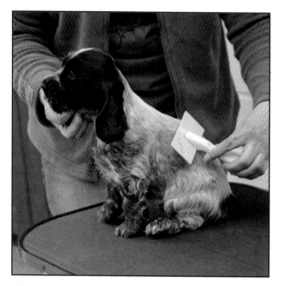

Give your puppy a gentle brush so that he gets used to sitting still while you groom him.

Pick up each paw in turn.

Check the ears. This is especially important with breeds such as the Cocker Spaniel, which have long ears lying close to the head.

With practice, your pup will allow you to examine his teeth and gums.

WEARING A COLLAR

It is a good idea to get your puppy used to wearing a collar which will give you some measure of control. It is also important that your pup accepts his collar before you start lead training. To begin with, choose a soft, lightweight collar that your pup will scarcely notice. He will quickly out-grow this, so replace it with a nylon adjustable collar, which you can extend as your puppy grows.

Most puppies quickly get used to wearing a collar. The best plan is to put it on just before a meal, so that your pup has something else to think about. He may scratch at it periodically, but it will not take long before he ignores it-. It is better to keep the collar on all the time, even if your pup is scratching at it, otherwise he will not become accustomed to wearing it.

The one exception to this is when you put your puppy in his crate, as discussed earlier.

PLAYING WITH TOYS

Playing with a pup is a good way of providing fun and tiring him out, as well as spending time interacting with him. There is no shortage of dog toys on the market, but which are the most suitable for a puppy?

When your pup first arrives in his new home, it is hard to believe that he has the power to destroy. But even though he only has milk teeth, a puppy can inflict a fair amount of damage on his toys. When he is teething, usually at around four months, his gums will be very tender, and most puppies become even more addicted to chewing at this stage. Some adult dogs grow out of chewing and take good care of their toys, but there are plenty of others who will have a go at destroying any toy on offer.

It is important to find toys that are 100 per cent safe – particularly if your pup is unsupervised, such as when you leave him with a toy in his crate. If a pup swallows part of a toy, it could have lethal consequences.

TOYS TO AVOID

- Soft toys that have glass eyes – these will be bitten off in no time.
- Squeaky toys. Dogs love these, but it is all too easy to bite through the plastic and get at the squeaker. If you provide squeaky toys, they should only be allowed when your dog is being carefully supervised.
- Old shoes or slippers. You might have no further use for an old slipper, but a pup will not distinguish between old and new. You will be furious if he gets hold of your new shoes, but is he really to blame?

SAFE TOYS

- Toys made of hard rubber, which is virtually indestructible.
- Rubber Kongs. These are made of hard rubber and can also be filled with food to provide a boredom-busting toy when you need to leave your pup.
- Raggers. These come in different shapes and sizes, and are good for tug games. However, be careful of playing this type of game when your puppy is teething, as it could be uncomfortable for him, and it

Provide safe toys that are suitable for the size and strength of your dog.

could also damage his new teeth as they start to come through.

TEACHING MANNERS WITH TOYS
Puppies love to play, but it is all too easy for a pup to get over-excited and for a game to get out of hand.

When you are playing with your puppy, teach him to play in an acceptable manner. This is particularly important with children, when a play session can quickly escalate out of control.

- Make sure you start the game, and you decide when to finish it.

In this way, the puppy learns that you are in control of his toys.
- Do not encourage games that involve jumping up for the toy, or chasing when you are holding the toy.
- A game of tug is OK, as long as the pup does not become too

boisterous – or starts to growl as he tries to 'win' the toy. If you have a breed with a strong guarding instinct, such as a Rottweiler or a German Shepherd Dog, tug games are best avoided.

- Chase games, such as running after a ball, are OK, but take care if you have a breed such as a Border Collie, with a strong inherited instinct to chase and herd. If you strengthen this instinct, you may well end up with a dog that is completely ball obsessed.

- Make sure your puppy will give up his toy on request and will let you take it without jumping up or trying to grab it back. (See Retrieve training, page 135).

- Avoid rough and tumble games, particularly if you have a puppy that is going to grow into a large dog. These games are very confusing for a puppy and teach nothing but bad habits, such as jumping up and mouthing. However, the greatest danger is that the pup sees you as a playmate, or even a rival, rather than a leader he must respect.

HOUSE RULES

In order for a puppy to find a place in the family pack, he needs to learn some basic house rules – and you should start teaching these from day one. A pup does not arrive in a new home knowing that he is not allowed on the furniture, or that he should not jump up when you are eating – he has to be

When you play with your dog, make sure you are in control of the game.

You can teach your dog to give up his toy by swapping it for a treat.

It is important to establish house rules so your puppy understands what is acceptable behaviour.

shown what is acceptable and what is not.

The first step is for you to decide what house rules you are going to impose, and then get the whole family to co-operate. If you correct your puppy for jumping up, and someone else in the family lets him get away with it, you will end up with a very confused puppy.

Every family and every household is different, but here are some house rules that you may want to consider:

• Is your puppy allowed free access to all rooms, or do you want to put up baby-gates to limit where he goes?
• Do you want to stop your puppy

climbing on to the furniture?
• Do you want to stop your puppy sleeping on your bed?
• Do you want to ban your puppy from family mealtimes until he learns to leave you alone?

In all cases, you need to impose the rules consistently so that your puppy knows what he is allowed to do. If he tries to jump on the sofa, for example, correct him by saying "No" in a firm voice, and then give him lots of praise for responding to you. Remember, if your pup has never been allowed to go on the sofa or sleep on your bed, he will find it much easier to comply with your wishes. The key is to teach

your puppy good habits from the moment he arrives in his new home. Your pup will thrive on being given clear leadership, and will respect you as his leader and provider.

TAKING ON A RESCUED DOG
If you are taking on an adult rescued dog, you will still need to spend time helping the dog to settle into his new home in much the same way as you would with a puppy. In most cases an adult will already be familiar with a home environment, and many will be house trained. However, the stress of moving homes means that house training can break down,

and you may need to go back to basics to re-educate your dog.

Hopefully, you will have some knowledge of the dog's background, but it is wise to proceed with caution, introducing him slowly and tactfully to each new situation. In this way you can monitor his reactions and keep a check on his anxiety levels. It is also important to establish house rules right from the beginning. An adult dog who has lived with another family may have been given different rules – or no rules at all – so you need to show him where his boundaries lie.

In some cases, a rescued dog may have some behavioural problems due to lack of training, or it may be that he has not been properly socialised. Advice is given on these issues in Chapter Five, but if you feel you are failing to cope, do not delay in calling in an expert. Your vet can put you in touch with an animal behaviourist if this seems to be the best course of action.

Be kind and patient with your new dog, but make sure you are consistent in everything you do. A dog with a past history desperately needs to feel safe and secure, and the sooner he understands what is expected of him, the sooner he will settle into his new home.

If you take on an adult rescued dog, he will need time to adjust to his new home.

Find out as much as possible about your dog's background so you can help him to settle more quickly.

THE IMPORTANCE OF SOCIALISATION

Chapter 5

When a puppy is settling into his new home, he will be confronted with a whole range of different experiences and situations. This starts with meeting his new family and becoming familiar with the home environment, and then, when he has completed his vaccinations, getting to grips with the outside world.

The process of learning through experience is known as socialisation, and it is a crucial part of a dog's development. Your puppy is not only becoming a part of your home and family, he is becoming a member of the community. He needs to be able to live in the outside world, coping calmly with every new situation that comes his way. It is your job to introduce him to as many different experiences as possible, and encourage him to behave in an appropriate manner.

In order to socialise your puppy effectively, it is helpful to understand how his brain is developing. Then you will get a perspective on how he sees the world.

PHASES OF SOCIALISATION

CANINE SOCIALISATION (BIRTH TO 7 WEEKS)

This is the time when a dog learns how to be a dog. By interacting with his mother and his littermates, a young pup learns about leadership and submission. He learns to read body posture so that he understands the intentions of his mother and his siblings. A puppy that is taken away from his litter too early may always have behavioural problems with other dogs, either being fearful or aggressive.

SOCIALISATION PERIOD (7 TO 12 WEEKS)

This is the time to get cracking and introduce your puppy to as many different experiences as possible. This includes meeting different people, other dogs and animals, seeing new sights, and hearing a range of sounds, from the vacuum cleaner to the roar of traffic. At this stage, a puppy learns very quickly, and what he learns will stay with him for the rest of his life. This is the best time for a puppy to move to a new home, as he is adaptable and ready to form deep bonds.

Between 7 and 12 weeks a puppy will soak up new experiences like a sponge.

Puppies learn their first lessons from their mother and by interacting with their littermates.

Keep experiences positive in the fear-imprint period.

Be consistent in your role as leader during the seniority period when a pup will start to question his status.

FEAR-IMPRINT PERIOD
(8 TO 11 WEEKS)

This occurs during the socialisation period, and it can be the cause of problems if it is not handled carefully. If a pup is exposed to a frightening or painful experience, it will make a lasting impression. Obviously, you will attempt to avoid frightening situations, such as your pup being bullied by a mean-spirited older dog, or a firework going off, but you cannot always protect your puppy from the unexpected. If your pup has a nasty experience, the best plan is to make light of it and distract him by offering him a treat or a game. The pup will take the lead from you and will be reassured that there is nothing to worry about. If you mollycoddle him and sympathise with him, he is far more likely to retain the memory of his fear.

SENIORITY PERIOD
(12 TO 16 WEEKS)

During this period, your puppy starts to cut the apron strings and becomes more independent. He will test out his status to find out who is the pack leader: him or you. Bad habits, such as play biting, which may have been seen as endearing a few weeks earlier, should be firmly discouraged. Remember to use positive, reward-based training, but make sure your puppy knows that you are the leader and must be respected.

SECOND FEAR-IMPRINT PERIOD
(6 TO 14 MONTHS)

This period is not as critical as the first fear-imprint period, but it should still be handled carefully. During this time your puppy may appear apprehensive, or he may show fear of something familiar. You may feel as if you have taken a backwards step, but if you adopt a

It is essential that the more assertive breeds, such as the Rottweiler, fully understand their place in the family pack.

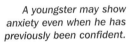

A youngster may show anxiety even when he has previously been confident.

calm, positive manner, your puppy will see that there is nothing to be frightened of. Do not make your dog confront the thing that frightens him. Simply distract his attention, and give him something else to think about, such as obeying a simple command – "Sit" or "Down". This will give you the opportunity to praise and reward your dog, and will help to boost his confidence.

YOUNG ADULTHOOD AND MATURITY (1 TO 4 YEARS)
The timing of this phase depends on the size of the dog: the bigger the dog, the later it is. This period coincides with a dog's increased size and strength, mental as well as physical.

Some dogs, particularly those with a more assertive nature, will test your leadership again and may become aggressive towards other dogs. Firmness and continued training are essential at this time so that your dog accepts his status in the family pack.

HOME ENVIRONMENT
If your puppy has been reared in the breeder's home rather than in a kennel environment, you will start with a big advantage. Your puppy will already be familiar with household sights and sounds, and he will be used to being handled by different people.

Some breeders who use kennels work very hard at socialising their puppies, bringing them into the house and handling them on a regular basis. However, kennel-reared puppies are likely to be more backward in terms of their early education than home-reared puppies. If you have taken on a rescued dog, he may have been poorly socialised and you will need to treat him as you would a young puppy.

A puppy has to learn to make decisions without the support of his littermates.

Regardless of your dog's background, it is a good idea to spend some time familiarising him with his home environment, so that you can be on hand to encourage him and too boost his confidence if he shows fear or apprehension of anything.

Introduce your puppy to the following:

- Vacuum cleaner
- Television
- Washing machine
- Spin dryer
- Dishwasher

Adopt the following procedure:

- Start with the machine switched off, and call your puppy over to you. Most puppies will take little notice of an inanimate object, so you can simply make a game of calling him over, and then reward him with a treat.
- If your pup is suspicious, give him lots of verbal encouragement, making sure you sound bright and positive. Remember, you are teaching him there is nothing to fear, not giving him the sympathy vote. When he

responds, give him lots of praise and reward him with a treat.

- If your pup has shown any anxiety, do not attempt to progress too quickly. Keep working with the pup while the machine is turned off until he is completely relaxed. Try playing a game with a toy, as this will distract the puppy, and you will spend more time around the machine so that it loses its novelty value.
- When your puppy is happy and relaxed, try turning the machine

When a puppy arrives in his new home, he can feel overwhelmed by all the experiences he has to cope with.

on. Initially, this may startle the pup, so be on hand with a treat and lots of verbal praise. You can throw a few treats alongside the machine so that your pup has to go up close to the machine in order to get them. In most cases, the desire for food will win the day!

- If your pup tries to run away, stay calm and relaxed, and move away from the machine, calling your pup to you. You will find a spot where he feels safe, and then you can reward him with a treat or a game. Take time, and progress slowly, inching towards the machine until your pup is accustomed to it. Do not attempt this in a single training session. Keep repeating the lesson over a number of days until your puppy gains confidence.

- When you are getting your puppy used to the vacuum cleaner, do not switch it on and advance towards him. This can be very scary for the bravest of pups. You need to let the puppy get used to the noise first, and only start vacuuming when he is calm and relaxed.

In most cases, a puppy will learn to accept all household sights and sounds within a matter of days. However, if your puppy is nervous, or you have taken on a rescued dog that is showing signs of fear, do not give in. It is important that your puppy learns there is nothing to worry about in his home. Be kind and patient, but also be firm, showing your pup that there is no cause for alarm.

MEETING AND GREETING

It will not take long for your puppy to become part of the family circle, and he will bond and form a relationship with each of the family members. However, a pup also has to learn to accept visitors coming to the house, which involves meeting and greeting in a calm, confident manner.

Every household has a variety of visitors. Taking on a broad cross-section, your puppy will meet the following:

• Friends and relatives, covering a range of ages.
• Delivery personnel, which will include a daily delivery of post.
• Tradesmen, such as builders, plumbers and window cleaners.
• Refuse collectors.

A friendly, confident puppy will be delighted to meet anyone who comes to the house – the major problem will be curbing his enthusiasm. Try the following:

• When someone comes to the door, make sure you have the pup under control. If necessary, put him on his lead so you can prevent him jumping up.
• Give the visitor a treat, and ask them to greet the puppy – but only when he is sitting calmly.
• After a brief greeting, the pup can be rewarded with a treat. Again, make sure the pup has all four feet on the ground.

If you follow this procedure, the pup will learn that he will be given

A puppy has to learn acceptable greeting behaviour.

Broaden your puppy's horizons, but proceed at a pace that suits him.

attention without having to jump up and demand it. Sometimes a pup may show some suspicion; this is more likely to be the case if the visitor is wearing something unfamiliar, such as a hat, or is carrying a stick, or maybe a bag of tools. If your pup shows concern, do not force him to go up and greet the visitor. Give him some reassurance, without making a big fuss, and then continue talking to the visitor. This gives the pup time to assess the situation, and he will be able to tell from your demeanour that there is nothing to fear. In this situation, it is important to keep the lead attached so the pup can sit with you, rather than trying to run away.

If the puppy appears to relax after a few minutes, you can ask the visitor to offer a treat. In most cases, the puppy will have got over his anxiety and be happy to greet the visitor and take the treat. If the pup is still tense, do not force the issue. Let him watch and learn, and, even if he is not ready to be greeted this time, he will have learnt that there is no cause for concern. Repeat the scenario every time a visitor comes to the door, giving praise and encouragement, and your pup will gradually grow in confidence.

THE OUTSIDE WORLD

When your puppy has completed his vaccinations, he will be ready to venture into the outside world. This is a very exciting time for both dog and owner, so it is important to make new experiences positive and educational. All dogs are individuals, and you will need to progress at a pace that suits your own dog. If your puppy is bold and out-going, you can get started and expose him to a variety of situations. If your pup is a little apprehensive, or you are working with an older dog that may have been poorly socialised, you will

Start off socialising your puppy in a quiet residential area.

need to progress more slowly. The aim is for your dog to be calm and relaxed, taking all new situations in his stride.

PROGRAMME FOR SOCIALISATION

This will vary depending on where you live, but try to include as many of the venues listed below as possible.

- Start off in a quiet residential area so your puppy gets used to a low volume of traffic. He will see some people, possibly other dogs out walking on the lead,

dustbins and wheelie bins, parked cars, bicycles, and maybe the neighbourhood cat.
- Go to a school when it is dropping-off or picking-up time. This is especially important if you do not have young children at home. Here your pup will see lots of children, pushchairs, as well as cars stopping and starting.
- Go to a local park and watch children in the play area. You will not be able to take your puppy inside the play area, but he will see children playing and will get used to their shouts of excitement.

- Visit a town centre where there will be heavier traffic, buses and lorries. If your pup is concerned, keep him on the inside of the pavement so he is not so close to the traffic. If possible, find a seat, and spend a few minutes sitting and watching the world go by. This will give your pup a chance to assess what is going on without having to confront it.
- Attend puppy classes. These are designed for puppies between the ages of 12 to 20 weeks, and give puppies a chance to play and interact together in a controlled, supervised

A trip out to a country fair provides many useful lessons.

Use every opportunity to enhance your puppy's social education.

Meeting and greeting under controlled circumstances teaches a dog to inhibit his behaviour.

environment. Your vet will have details of a local class.

- Go on a walk with a friend or friends that have dogs of sound temperament. This will give your puppy the opportunity to play, and he will also learn how to behave around other dogs.
- Go to a railway station. You don't have to get on a train if you don't need to, but your puppy will have the chance to experience trains, people wheeling luggage, loudspeaker announcements, and going up and down stairs and over railway bridges.

- Visit a street market. There will be crowds of people, and a wide variety of stalls – those selling food will be especially enticing. You may also encounter other dogs and their owners, so your pup will learn to meet and greet when he is on a lead.
- If you live in the town, plan a trip to the country. You can enjoy a day out and provide an opportunity for your puppy to see livestock, such as sheep, cattle and horses.
- One of the best places for socialising a dog is at a country

fair. There will be crowds of people, livestock in pens, tractors, bouncy castles, fairground rides and food stalls.
- When your dog is over 20 weeks of age, track down a training class for adult dogs. You may find that your local training class has both puppy and adult classes.

TRAINING CLUBS

There are lots of training clubs to choose from. Your vet will probably have details of clubs in your area, or you can ask friends who have

A well-run class will provide the benefits of both training and socialisation.

dogs if they attend a club. Alternatively, use the Internet to find out more information. But how do you know how good the club is?

Before you take your dog, ask if you can go to a class as an observer and find out the following:

- What experience does the instructor(s) have?
- Is the instructor a member of the Association of Pet Dogs Trainers? This organisation is committed to improving the standard of training and education, and membership will give some guarantee of the instructor's experience and commitment.
- Do any of the instructors have experience with your breed?
- Is the class well organised, and are the dogs reasonably quiet? (A noisy class indicates an unruly atmosphere, which will not be conducive to learning).
- Are there are a number of classes to suit dogs of different ages and abilities?
- Are positive, reward-based training methods used?
- Does the club train for the Good Citizen Scheme (see page 151).

If you are not happy with the training club, find another one. An inexperienced instructor who cannot handle a number of dogs in a confined environment can do more harm than good.

SETTING UP FOR SUCCESS

Chapter 6

earning needs to be a positive experience for both teacher and pupil, so how do you go about finding the best training environment and the most effective training methods? The top priorities are to find a reward that your dog really values, and to open up clear channels of communication (see Chapter Three: Tools of the Trade). The next step is to work out what you want to achieve from your training sessions. Learning is a gradual, on-going process, so you need to set clear objectives to give you and your dog the best possible chance of success.

GETTING STARTED

- Find a training area that is free from distractions, particularly when you are just starting out.
- Keep training sessions brief,

Select a favourite toy and only bring it out when you are training.

especially with a young puppy. He has a very short attention span.

- Do not train if you are in a bad mood or if you are on a tight schedule – the training session will be doomed to failure.
- If you are using a toy as a reward, make sure it is only available when you are training. In this way it has an added value for your dog.
- If you are using food treats, make sure they are bite-size

and easy to swallow; you don't want to hang about while your dog chews on his treat.

- All food treats must be deducted from your dog's daily food ration.
- When you are training, move around your allocated area so that your dog does not think that an exercise can only be performed in one place.
- If your dog is finding an exercise difficult, try not to get frustrated.

Go back a step and praise him for his effort. You will probably find he is more successful when you try again at the next training session.

- Always end sessions on a happy, positive note. Ask your dog to do something you know he can do – it could be a trick he enjoys performing – and then reward him with a few treats or a longer tug on his toy, so your dog knows you are pleased with him.

Your dog will pick up on your body language and this will help him to learn.

YOUR ROLE

When you start training, you need to tune into your dog and find a way of teaching him so he can pick up your signals quickly and easily. Training breaks down when a dog is confused about what you want and then becomes stubborn or worried because he does not know what to do.

Bear in mind the following points:

- **Be consistent:** Train each exercise in the same sequence, using the same cues/commands.
- **Give one command only:** If you keep repeating a command, or keeping changing it, your dog will think you are babbling and will probably ignore you. If your dog does not respond the first time you ask, make it simple by using a treat to lure him into position, and then you can reward him for a correct response.

- **Get your timing right:** If you are rewarding your dog and equally if you are reprimanding him, you must respond within one to two seconds otherwise the dog will not link his behaviour with your reaction (see Chapter Three).
- **Read your dog's body language:** Be observant, reading your dog's body language and facial expressions so that you understand his feelings and his intentions.
- **Be aware of your own body language:** You can help your dog to learn by using your body language to communicate with him (see Chapter Three). Remember, a dog has an uncanny knack of knowing your moods and your intentions before you have given out any obvious signals. For this reason, you must always try to keep one

step ahead, and try to see the world from your dog's perspective.
- **Tone of voice:** Dogs are very receptive to tone of voice, so use this to your advantage, and give praise and encouragement.

CLICKER TRAINING

Positive, reward-based training is the key to success, but you may want to have a go at clicker training, which gives you an extra tool when you are using these methods.

Animal behaviourist Karen Pryor pioneered the technique of clicker training when she was working with dolphins. Karen wanted to mark 'correct' behaviour at the precise moment it happened. She found it was impossible to toss a fish to a dolphin in mid-air, when she wanted to reward it. Her aim was

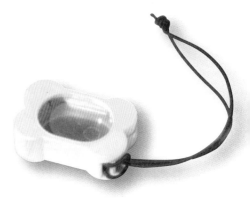

to establish a conditioned response so the dolphin knew that it had performed correctly and a reward would follow.

The solution was the clicker: a small matchbox-shaped training aid, with a metal tongue that makes a click when it is pressed. To begin with, the dolphin had to learn that a click meant that food was coming. The dolphin then learnt that it must 'earn' a click in order to get a reward. Clicker training has been used with many different animals, most particularly with dogs, and it has proved hugely successful. It is a great aid for pet owners and is also widely used by professional trainers who are training highly specialised skills.

INTRODUCING A CLICKER

This is easy and a dog who is food motivated will learn about the clicker in record time! It can be combined with attention training, which is a very useful tool and can be used on many different occasions.

- Prepare some treats and go to an area that is free from distractions. When your dog stops sniffing around and looks at you, click and reward by throwing him a treat. This means he will not crowd you, but will go looking for the treat. Repeat a couple of times. If your dog is very easily distracted, you may need to start this exercise with the dog on a lead.
- After a few clicks, your dog will understand that if he hears a

click, he will get a treat. He must now learn that he must 'earn' a click. This time, when your dog looks at you, wait a little longer before clicking, and then reward him. If your dog is on a lead but responding well, try him off the lead.

- When your dog is working for a click and giving you his attention, you can introduce a cue word, such as "Watch".

It does not take a dog long to learn that he must earn a click in order to get a reward.

10 CLICKER TRAINING TIPS

The beauty of the clicker is that anyone can use it, but it will be more effective if you follow a few simple rules.

1 Wait until your dog has produced the correct behaviour before you produce a treat. The secret of the clicker is that it marks the exact moment that the dog has done the 'right' thing, and he will therefore associate this behaviour with hearing the click, and will be more likely to repeat it. The treat follows after the click, and your dog will soon learn this sequence.

2 Only click once. It is easy to get carried away and do multiple clicks if you are especially pleased with your dog's behaviour. This will only confuse your dog because he needs to hear a single click at the exact moment that he is doing as you ask.

3 A clicker-trained dog will respond as soon as he hears a click, but never use the clicker as a means of getting your dog's attention, or to signal him to come to you. It may work on the first few occasions, but it will soon become useless, as the click is not conveying any information to the dog.

4 Get your timing right. Don't click the dog as he is going in to the Down, or as he starts to get up. You need to click at the precise moment that your dog is in the Down so that he knows this behaviour has earned a click.

5 Only click the behaviour you want. Do not use the clicker to "gee up" your dog, encouraging him to walk to heel, for example. He must be clicked when he is walking to heel at your side, and you can reward him for giving the behaviour you want.

Repeat a few times, using the cue. You now have a dog that understands the clicker and will give you his attention when you ask him to "Watch".

Once you have established that your dog understands the clicker, you can introduce it to your training sessions. If your dog is toy orientated, you can still use the clicker, and then reward your dog with a game. He will quickly learn that a click means "OK", and he will know that a game will follow.

PROGRESSING IN STAGES
There are a number of exercises that involve several steps or stages. For example, when you are teaching a Recall, you will want

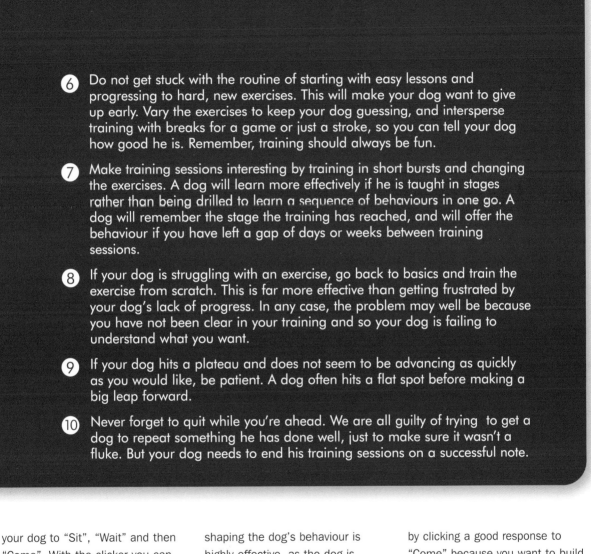

6 Do not get stuck with the routine of starting with easy lessons and progressing to hard, new exercises. This will make your dog want to give up early. Vary the exercises to keep your dog guessing, and intersperse training with breaks for a game or just a stroke, so you can tell your dog how good he is. Remember, training should always be fun.

7 Make training sessions interesting by training in short bursts and changing the exercises. A dog will learn more effectively if he is taught in stages rather than being drilled to learn a sequence of behaviours in one go. A dog will remember the stage the training has reached, and will offer the behaviour if you have left a gap of days or weeks between training sessions.

8 If your dog is struggling with an exercise, go back to basics and train the exercise from scratch. This is far more effective than getting frustrated by your dog's lack of progress. In any case, the problem may well be because you have not been clear in your training and so your dog is failing to understand what you want.

9 If your dog hits a plateau and does not seem to be advancing as quickly as you would like, be patient. A dog often hits a flat spot before making a big leap forward.

10 Never forget to quit while you're ahead. We are all guilty of trying to get a dog to repeat something he has done well, just to make sure it wasn't a fluke. But your dog needs to end his training sessions on a successful note.

your dog to "Sit", "Wait" and then "Come". With the clicker you can train in small steps, marking your dog's correct response and rewarding him before progressing to the next. This method of breaking down an exercise and shaping the dog's behaviour is highly effective, as the dog is continually motivated and rewarded rather than becoming frustrated by being asked too much at one time. So when you are training a Recall, you may start by clicking a good response to "Come" because you want to build on the dog's enthusiasm. You may then train a "Sit' and a Wait" separately so your dog is rock steady before putting the whole exercise together.

STATIONARY EXERCISES

Chapter 7

When you start working on a training programme, it is essential to bear in mind that all dogs are individuals and will progress at different rates. This not only depends on breed type, which may influence willingness to learn and aptitude for specific exercises, but just as importantly, the dog's age, temperament and background.

A young pup who has been well socialised from birth onwards is likely to be an eager pupil. An older dog that has been rehomed may be worried and anxious and may find it hard to focus on training before he has fully settled in his new home.

Work hard at evaluating your dog – his likes and dislikes, what motivates him, and what distracts him – and then you can fine-tune your training sessions to get the best out of your dog.

In this chapter, we will look at the first exercises you will teach your dog, which are known as the stationary exercises, as they are done on the spot. As always, positive, reward-based training methods are used. These can be taught with or without a clicker, depending on your personal preference. Equally, the exercises can be taught using a toy or a treat as a reward.

When you are teaching the stationary exercises, which include Sit, Down and Stand, you may find

it easier to use a treat to lure your dog into position. But if your dog is focused on his toy, this can also be used as a lure.

SIT

This is the easiest exercise to teach and you can start teaching it the moment your puppy arrives home. If you are training an older dog, he will probably respond to "Sit", but it will do no harm to give him a refresher lesson. It is rewarding for both you and your dog to get off to a good start.

- Choose a tasty treat and hold it just above your puppy's nose. As he looks up at the treat, he will naturally go into the Sit. As soon as he is in position, click and reward him. It does not matter if your dog gets up to take the treat, but he must be sitting

when you click him.
- Repeat the exercise a couple of times, giving lots of verbal praise when your dog responds correctly.
- At the next training session, your dog will probably go straight into a Sit as soon as he sees you holding out the treat. When you are confident that your dog understands what you want and is responding without hesitation, introduce the verbal cue "Sit". Give lots of praise and reward with a treat.
- With practice, your dog will respond to the verbal cue and you will not need to lure him into position.
- Remember to reinforce this lesson at mealtimes. You will find that your dog goes into the Sit in record time when you are holding out his food bowl!

BREED TIP

There are some breeds, such as Greyhounds, Lurchers, and other sighthounds, that find it uncomfortable to Sit for long periods. The same applies to the low-slung Dachshund. If your dog finds that sitting is not a natural position for him, use this exercise only when you need to. You may find that your dog is happier in the Stand, and this can be his principal stationary position.

TRAINING TIP

It is useful if you have a verbal cue to release your dog when an exercise is finished. This will help him to understand that he must stay in position until you say so. You can choose whatever word you like; many trainers opt for "OK" or "Finish". This gives the signal that the execise has been completed and a reward will follow.

Reward your dog on a random basis once he has learnt an exercise.

RANDOM REWARDS

How often should you reward your dog for a correct response? This can be a stumbling block, as you want to keep training positive, but you don't want a dog who is constantly mugging you for treats.

When you are first teaching an exercise, your dog needs all the encouragement you can give him, and he should be rewarded every time he gets it right. However, in a simple exercise, such as Sit, there is no need to reward your dog every time he sits on cue. If you think of it in human terms, you would praise a child the first time he/she said the first three letters of the alphabet. But would you give the same praise in six months' time if the child was still repeating "A, B, C"? If you did, the praise would be meaningless because it has involved no effort on the child's part. Instead, you would reserve your praise for when the child made significant progress: getting halfway through the alphabet, getting the whole way through, and then starting to read whole words.

In the same way, a dog must understand that he must work for his rewards. Once he has mastered a simple exercise, such as Sit, he can progress to do a Stay or a Recall before he gets a reward. However, it is important to keep your dog guessing so that he is motivated to keep on trying. For this reason, trainers use a system of random rewards. In most cases a simple "Sit" will not warrant a reward, but every fifth or sixth time, the dog is rewarded for a prompt response. This keeps the dog on his toes, and he is not likely to switch off because he is not being rewarded.

Keep a clenched fist so your dog can smell the treat but cannot get at it.

DOWN

Work hard at this exercise, because a reliable Down is useful in many different situations. It gives you excellent control over your dog, and you can build this up when you progress to teaching him to "Stay".

Lower a treat towards the ground, and your dog should follow it.

- You can start with your dog in a Sit, but you can teach it just as effectively when the dog is standing. Hold a treat just below your dog's nose, and slowly lower it towards the ground. The treat acts as a lure, and your dog will follow it, first going down on his forequarters, and then bringing his hindquarters down as he tries to get the treat.
- The moment your dog goes into the Down, click him. You may have to be quick, as some puppies are very wriggly.

When your dog readily goes into the Down, wait a few moments before rewarding him, so he learns to stay in position.

TRAINING TIP

In most cases, a dog will learn to go into the Down by following the lure, but if you are not careful, he will get stuck and only go into position when he is following the lure. The best plan is to go for a halfway house and introduce a hand signal, pointing your finger towards the floor. Your dog should follow this, and you can then click and reward. With practice, you can dispense with the hand signal and your dog will respond to the verbal cue.

For information on teaching the Instant Down, see Chapter 10: Advanced Exercises.

Hold a treat close to your dog's nose and lure your dog into the Stand.

- Make sure you close your fist around the treat, and only reward your puppy when you have clicked him for being in the correct position.
- If your puppy is reluctant to go Down, you can apply gentle pressure on his shoulders to encourage him to go into the correct position.
- When your puppy is following the treat and going into position, introduce a verbal cue.
- Build up this exercise over a period of time, each time waiting a little longer before giving the click, so the puppy learns to stay in the Down position. Remember to use your release word when the exercise is finished.

STAND

This exercise is often neglected, as it may not seem as useful as Sit and Down. However, life is much easier if you have a dog that will "Stand" on cue when you need to groom him, or if he needs to be examined by a vet.

- Start by putting your dog in a Sit, and show him that you have a treat in your hand.
- Draw your hand away from the dog's nose in a straight line, and your dog should follow it, going into the Stand. You can then click and reward.
- Make sure you do not move your hand too quickly, or your dog will walk towards the lure rather than going into the Stand position.
- Keep practising until your dog understands what you want. You can then introduce the verbal cue "Stand".
- Keep working on this exercise, gradually increasing the amount of time he stays in the "Stand" before you click and reward.

TRAINING TIP

If your dog is reluctant to go into the Stand, or keeps trying to Sit when you are luring him, you can give a little assistance. Place your hand on your dog's underside (see photo below), and gently stroke. This helps the dog to maintain the Stand and will help him to understand that this is the position you want. With practice, your dog will respond to the lure, and then to the verbal cue, and you can withdraw the helping hand.

LEAD WALKING

Chapter 8

Walking your dog on a loose lead does not seem a difficult goal to achieve – but it is an aspect of training that many owners struggle with. A young puppy misbehaving on the lead may not seem like the end of a world, but if you have a big, powerful dog, such as a Rottweiler, towing you across the park, lead walking soon ceases to be a pleasure. The secret of achieving success on the lead is to get off to a positive start. Lead walking should be seen as quality time when your dog is interacting with you – not a battle of wills when the strongest comes off best.

THE RIGHT START

A puppy is ripe for absorbing new experiences, and even though you cannot venture into the outside world until the vaccination programme has been completed, you can use the time to practise lead walking at home.

- The first step is to get your pup used to wearing a collar, which is one of the first lessons to teach when a pup arrives in his new home (see Chapter Four).
- Take your puppy into the garden, or select a room that is not too cluttered with furniture, and attach the lead.
- Initially let your puppy wander where he wants, but make sure the lead does not become tangled.
- Next, call your pup to you and reward him with a treat. This may be enough for the first lead training session. The aim is for the pup to move around freely without worrying about his lead.
- At your next training session, repeat the steps above to remind your puppy what he has already learnt. This time when he comes to you, pick up the lead and follow your pup wherever he wants to go. Do not try to control his movements at this stage. He is learning to accept the restraint of being held on the lead.
- Allow your pup to wander at will until you are confident that he has accepted the lead. Give him lots of praise when he is moving freely, and reward him.

TAKING CONTROL

When your puppy has accepted the lead and is used to being held and followed, it is time to introduce

To begin with, follow your pup wherever he wants to go.

With practice, your pup will learn to walk on a loose lead.

TRAINING TIP

If you are training a pet dog, the aim is to have a dog that walks by your side on a loose lead, giving you attention when you ask. This is very different from the position required in Competitive Obedience when the dog is glued to the handler's left side and gives total attention.

However, if you have taught your dog the cue to "Watch", you can start off by asking for your dog's attention, and then use the cue periodically if you want your dog's attention during the course of a walk. This may come in handy if you see another dog, or a neighbourhood cat, and you want your dog to focus on you. This will give you a strong measure of control, and you are asking your dog to do something positive which he will be rewarded for, rather than allowing him to follow his own desires.

some control so that the pup goes where you want him to go.

- Arm yourself with some treats and encourage your dog to follow your hand. To begin with, your pup will only focus on you for a few steps, but reward this behaviour with a click and a treat.
- Try again, this time walking in the opposite direction, encouraging your dog to walk with you. Only click him when he is walking on a loose lead by your side. You will have to be quick with the clicker, because your pup will only manage a few paces, but it is vital to click the behaviour you want.
- Introduce some circles as well as changes of direction so that your puppy gets used to walking alongside you.
- Lead walking is a matter of practice – and the more you

practise, the more quickly your pup will get the message and understand where he should be walking. Do not introduce the verbal cue "Heel" or "Close" until your pup is in the correct position.

- By tradition, dogs are trained to walk on the left-hand side. If you have plans to compete with your dog, it is important to work at this. To begin with, your pup will not be consistent, and will keep trying to change sides. When this happens, stand still and use a treat to get his attention. Then bring him back to the left-hand side and continue walking.

PULLING AHEAD

A bold, confident puppy may try to get in front of you simply because he is excited and wants to explore

his environment. You need to work at this from an early stage or it will quickly become an ingrained habit.

- When your pup pulls ahead, stand still. Get his attention and call him back to your left-hand side. It may help if you take a step back with your left foot to guide him into position. Now set off again. If you achieve a few paces with your dog walking on a loose lead in the correct position, click and reward.
- You can also try turning a small circle or walking in the opposite direction for a few paces. This will help your pup to learn that pulling ahead is non-productive; far from speeding things up, he has slowed to a halt – or gone in the opposite direction – so pulling ahead has not worked as a strategy.
- Progress may be slow, but if

A dog who is a persistent puller can make your life a misery, particularly if you own a large, powerful breed.

When your dog pulls, come to a complete standstill.

Get your dog's attention and call him back to your side.

You are now ready to continue your walk – and your dog has learnt that pulling has been non-productive because it has delayed his progress.

TRAINING TIP

If you have a dog that is not enjoying his lead work – either pulling ahead or lagging behind – introduce some changes of pace. If you have a dog that pulls, slow down and walk in long, measured strides, then speed up before going back to normal pace. This will keep your dog guessing and he will not become one-paced – i.e. pulling ahead of you. Equally, changes of pace will work with a dog that lags behind, as it introduces an element of surprise. A dog who is constantly having to adjust his pace will become focused and motivated, and will enjoy interacting with you.

you click and reward when you get the behaviour you want – and come to a halt when your pup is pulling – he will gradually learn which behaviour works for him.

LAGGING BEHIND

If there's one thing worse than the pup that pulls ahead, it is the one that lags behind. This may be because a pup is fearful and does not have the confidence to walk alongside you, or it may be that he resents the lead and does not want to co-operate with you.

- If you have a reluctant lead walker, it may help if you produce some really tasty treats, such as some sausage or cheese, which may help to persuade your dog that walking with you is a good idea.
- Start off in a positive style, making your voice sound bright and breezy so your pup thinks

he is going for a fun outing rather than a drill session. Encourage him with a treat, and be quick to click and reward if you get a couple of paces where the pup is walking beside you.

- If your pup starts to lag, or if he digs his heels in and refuses to budge, do not get confrontational. If your pup is being stubborn, he will be even more determined not to co-operate if he sees you becoming angry.
- The best plan is to go back to your pup's side, and then make a sharp change of direction. This will confuse your pup, because he had decided the way ahead was a no-go area and now you are setting off in the opposite direction. This should be enough to change your pup's mindset, and the second he is walking with you, click and reward.
- Keep repeating the above, never

giving in to your puppy, and never becoming frustrated by your lack of progress. Be generous with your praise – and with your rewards – when he gets it right, and he will learn that walking with you is a better option than going on a sit-down strike.

- If your pup is really stubborn and refuses to budge, try a different exercise, such as asking him to go into a Down. Again, this changes the mindset, and the pup is co-operating with you – even though it is not exactly the behaviour you want! However, you have the opportunity to praise and reward him, rather than getting stuck with non co-operation. You can now try lead walking again, and your pup will see it as a whole new exercise rather than a continuation of an old battle.

What do you do if your dog refuses to budge?

Use lots of verbal encouragement and produce a really tasty treat to get your dog moving.

Try some changes of direction and changes of pace to motivate your dog.

TRAINING TIP

If you are having problems with lead training, try using a toy to motivate your dog. If you break up lead walking with a game of tug, or if you let your dog have his favourite squeaky toy for a quick play, he will start to see the lesson as fun. When you stop playing, your pup will know you have the toy, and he will focus his attention on you. You can then walk a few paces with the pup at your side, giving his attention to you, before rewarding him with a click and then breaking off for another game. Again, progress will be slow, but it is far better to mark and reward the behaviour you want rather than being stuck with a dog that never learns to walk on a loose lead.

TRAINING AIDS

If you have taken on an older dog that has not been trained to walk on the lead, you may have to start from scratch, teaching him the basics so that he understands the behaviour you want. However, you may have a dog that has got into the habit of pulling on the lead, and this can be a considerable challenge – particularly with large breeds.

It is important to try all the measures outlined above – which will work in time – but you may also need a little extra help. There are now a number of training aids on the market, and these will help your dog to stop pulling. This will give you the opportunity to reward him, and he will start to learn that it is more beneficial to him than pulling ahead.

HARNESS

It may be beneficial to try walking your dog on a harness. This has the advantage of preventing strangulation sensations around the neck caused by persistent pulling, and therefore puts an end to unpleasant associations triggered by lead walking. This effectively gives you and your dog a fresh start, and you can teach him to enjoy walking alongside you. Many owners have also found that their dogs are less stressed walking on a harness as it gives them freedom of movement and posture, which can help when they meet other dogs and are trying to communicate with them.

It is important that the harness is well fitted and has padded straps. This changes the dog's centre of gravity by evenly distributing his weight around his shoulders. The dogs is more balanced, and will not

suffer injury or discomfort that can result from a dog that continually pulls on the collar and lead.

HEAD COLLAR

This works on the same principle as a horse's head collar. Most dogs object to a head collar the first time it is fitted, but it does not take long before the equipment is accepted. If your dog fusses at his head collar, and tries to paw at it, distract his attention by having a game with him, or asking him to do a simple exercise, such as a Sit, so you can reward him.

The advantage of the head collar is that the dog can no longer pull from the neck, which is an ingrained habit with persistent pullers. The pressure from a head collar comes over the muzzle area, and the very fact that you have broken the cycle of pulling from the neck will help enormously.

Remember to work at teaching your dog the Heel position, and, with practice, he will understand where he should be, and will not attempt to pull.

Some dogs need a head collar for a short amount of time while you are retraining. However, some dogs are more of a challenge, and it may be better to use the back of a head collar in order to achieve good heelwork – and to have a dog that is a pleasure to walk with.

A training aid, such as a control harness, will help you in the initial stages when you are trying to correct a pulling dog.

Once a dog has accepted a head collar, lead walking becomes more controlled.

STAY EXERCISES

Chapter 9

Teaching your dog to Stay may not seem the most exciting exercise, but you will never regret the work you put in. A dog with a reliable Stay is easy to control in the home, and you are more likely to take your dog out and about if you know you can trust him to Stay until you are ready to release him, or to put him back on the lead.

Ideally, you should teach your puppy to Stay as one of his first exercises. But if you have taken on an older dog, who has not learnt to Stay, do not despair. It is not too late to start, even though you may need extra patience. You can progress in exactly the same way as you would when training a puppy.

GIVING THE RIGHT CUE

Some trainers use the verbal command "Stay" when the dog is to

Stay in position for an extended period of time, and "Wait" if the dog is to remain in position for a few seconds until you give the next command. Others trainers use a universal "Stay" to cover all situations. It all comes down to personal preference, and as long as you are consistent, your dog will understand the command he is given.

EARLY TRAINING

You cannot start teaching your dog to Stay until he has perfected the Sit, and ideally the Down as well. In the initial stages it will help if your puppy is on a lead and this will give you more control.

• Position your dog at your left-hand side and ask him to go into the Sit/Down (use the position with which your dog is most secure). Take one pace to the side, wait a second, and step back. Click your dog when you have returned to

To begin with, keep your dog on the lead, and leave him just a few paces.

TRAINING TIP

Your dog will learn this exercise more quickly if you use a hand signal as you leave him in position. The clearest signal is to hold your palm flat towards the dog, so that it looks as though you are blocking his advance.

TRAINING TIP

Remember to keep your body very still when you are training this exercise, and avoid eye contact with your dog, as he will read this as an invitation to come to you.

his side, and then use your release word – "OK" /Finish" so he knows the exercise is finished. You can then reward your dog.

- Repeat this several times so that your dog understands that he must Stay in position. If he tries to get up, simply go back to him, put him back in the Sit/Down and repeat the exercise.
- Gradually increase the distance you leave your dog until he is at the end of his lead. Remember

to wait until you have returned to his side before you click, release and reward.

- Your dog should now understand that he must Stay in position, so introduce the verbal cue "Stay".

FACING YOUR DOG

- Repeat the early training exercise outlined above, but this time, stand and face your dog and take a step back. This may not seem to be an advance on early

training, but when you are facing your dog, you pose more of an invitation for him to get up and join you.

- Again, gradually increase the distance until your dog is at the end of his lead.

WORKING OFF-LEAD

When your dog is responding to the verbal cue "Stay", and is holding his position, it is time to try him off the lead. To begin with, simply drop

Build up the distance and the time you can leave your dog in the Stay.

the lead, and go no further than the end of the lead. This means that if your dog breaks his Stay, you can tread on the lead and halt his progress.

It may be easier to practise your first off-lead Stays in the house with the minimum of distractions. When your dog is proving reliable in the Stay, take him into the garden, and practise in a more challenging environment.

By now you should be practising Stay in both the Sit and the Down positions.

MAKING THE STAY ROCK STEADY

Once your dog is happy to Stay off the lead, the next step is to increase the distance you can leave your dog, and the amount of time you can leave him in the Stay. To achieve this, you need to work with your dog so that he becomes completely reliable.

- When you have asked your dog to "Stay", vary the routine so that he learns to remain in position, no matter what you are doing.
- Walk in a small circle around your dog, and then click, release and reward when you have returned to his left-hand side.
- Repeat the exercise, this time increasing the size of your circle.
- If your dog is on the Down, you can circle him and then step over him. This may well surprise him and make him break the Stay. But, with practice, he will understand that the verbal cue

"Stay" means that he must not move – even if you are stepping right over him!

- Face your dog and walk backwards for a few paces. Stand sideways on, and leave your dog in the Stay for approximately 20 seconds before going back to him.
- Try the same exercise again, but this time, bend and tie (or pretend to tie) your shoelace. The dog will be watching you like

a hawk, and he needs to learn that if you change your body language, it is not a signal for him to come to you. He must stay in position until you have released him. You can also try moving your hand up and down, or any other mock signals, so that your dog becomes rock steady in the Stay.

- Gradually build up the distance you can leave your dog, and work at building up the time, 20

Try circling round your dog to see if he can maintain his position.

Give a clear instruction when you leave your dog.

The big test comes when you walk away from your dog, leaving him in the Stay.

You may need to reinforce the Stay by using a hand signal.

Praise your dog in position before releasing him.

TRAINING TIP

If your dog makes a mistake in training, such as breaking a Stay, do not confuse him by telling him off or explaining what he has done wrong – your dog will have no idea what you are talking about. Instead, remain calm, so that you are giving off neutral vibes. You are not being positive and praising your dog; equally, you are not being negative and reprimanding him. You are simply showing your dog that this is not the behaviour you want. If you want to speak to your dog, a neutral "No" in a quiet tone of voice will suffice. Then place your dog back in position and repeat the exercise. When your dog gets it right, make an extra-special fuss of him, throwing in a few extra treats, or giving an extra-long play with his toy.

seconds at a time, until you can leave your dog for a full minute.

WALKING AWAY

You now have a dog that is reliable in the Stay – but can you trust him to remain in position if you turn your back on him? This is important if you are teaching a formal Recall (see page 130), but it is also a valuable exercise for everyday use.

When you are working on this exercise, you will need an observer who will tell if the dog has broken his Stay.

• Position your dog at your left-hand side and ask him to "Sit", and then tell him to "Stay".
• Set off with your right leg leading (which is furthest from the dog, and therefore less of a 'signal') and walk a few paces before returning to your dog's left-hand side. Click, release and reward.
• Keep repeating this exercise until your dog is confident enough to

stay in position. If he does break his Stay, put him back in position and start again.

STAND-STAY

When your dog is confident in both the Sit-Stay and the Down-Stay, you can introduce a Stand-Stay. This is not essential, but if you can get your dog to Stand and also to remain in position, it will be an advantage when you are grooming, or if your dog needs to be examined by a vet. In the show ring, dogs are taught to stand in show, so this exercise is

In the show ring a dog needs to maintain the Stand-Stay while the judge inspects him.

invaluable for all show-goers.

It is trained in exactly the same way as a Sit-Stay and a Down-Stay, but it is obviously more tempting for the dog to move when he is on his feet. The secret is to progress slowly, working on-lead until you are confident that your dog understands what you want. Reward frequently, and do not be too ambitious as to how long you leave your dog in position.

EXTENDED STAY

There are times when you want your dog to remain in position for an extended period of time, such as when you are having a drink with friends. This could be in someone's home, in a café or a pub if dogs are allowed, or sitting outside in a garden.

The aim is for the dog to "Settle" so that he is not being a nuisance, but it does not demand the concentration required for a formal Stay exercise.

In most situations, the dog will be asked to "Settle" on-lead, and the aim is for him to lie down quietly and "switch off" until it is time to go. As this name suggests, this exercise is simply an extension of the Stay exercise, and so you will need to do all the preliminary work outlined in this chapter.

To build up to an Extended Stay, try the following:

- Put your dog in the Down, making sure he has sufficient room to stretch out if he wants to.
- Now ignore your dog. This may seem harsh, but if you are fussing him or talking to him, he will want to interact with you. If you ignore him, he will learn to switch off, as nothing exciting is happening to him.
- If your dog seeks attention and shifts position, put him back in the Down, repeating the verbal cue. After a few minutes, reward your dog, but do so quietly and calmly so that he does not think it is time to get up and go.
- Make sure your dog has settled again for several minutes before

Practise the Extended Stay at home, and soon you will have a dog that will "Settle" when you take him out and meet with friends.

TRAINING TIP

You can practise the Extended Stay while watching TV. This is an ideal scenario, as you will be distracted by the television and so you will not pay any attention to the dog. In his home environment a dog is more likely to settle, and so this will get the exercise off to a flying start.

An impressive example of a Group Stay.

finishing the exercise.

- Gradually build up the amount of time you expect your dog to remain in position, and reward him only once or twice during that period.

- When you next try this exercise, reward him in the Down after a few minutes, and then introduce the verbal cue "Settle". Leave him for a little longer before finishing the exercise.

- At the next session, introduce the verbal cue "Settle" and your dog will realise that this is a different exercise from "Down", and all he needs to do is to lie down quietly until you give your next cue.

GROUP STAYS

If you attend a training club, or you go walking with friends who have dogs, you can have a go at a Group Stay. This is far from easy, as the dogs have to resist the temptation of making friends with their neighbours. Initially, train this exercise with the dogs in the Down, as this is generally a more secure position for them.

- Start off with the dogs on-lead, and the handlers can back away to the end of the dog's lead.

- Repeat the exercise, this time dropping leads.

- If the dogs are progressing well, repeat the exercise off-lead. You can also try a small circle around your dogs to reinforce the Stay.

- When your dogs are consistently remaining in position, try the final challenge of the handler walking away, waiting for 20 seconds, and then returning to the dogs. Again, you can build up the amount of time you leave the dogs until they can do a one-minute Stay.

ADVANCED EXERCISES

Chapter 10

By now you should have good control over your dog, so it is time to progress to exercises that are a little more challenging.

RECALL

A dog with a reliable Recall is a pleasure to own, as you can allow him to free run in the full knowledge that he will come back to you on cue. This means you can give your dog the freedom to run and play, meet new friends and investigate enticing scents without the stress of trying to catch him at the end of the walk. It is a goal that is well worth achieving, so the Recall exercise should be given a top priority in your training programme.

FIRST STEPS

A puppy has a natural instinct to follow: you can see this if you watch a litter of

puppies playing together. The pups will follow their mother, and if a bold pup runs off to investigate, the other pups will not be far behind. The breeder will have made use of this instinct, calling the puppies at mealtimes or to go in or out of the garden. You should build on this from the moment your puppy arrives home, calling him to you, and then giving lots of praise. You can also have a game with your pup to reinforce the Recall:

• Recruit a helper and take your pup into the garden.

Start working on the Recall from an early age when a puppy wants the security of being with you.

• Hold the pup while your helper walks some distance away.
• The helper calls the pup, "Come, Woodie", and you release him. The pup will head towards the helper and should be rewarded with lots of praise and a treat.
• Now reverse roles so that your helper holds the pup and you call him to you. In this way, your pup learns to respond to different people as well as enjoying a fun game.

BUILDING AN ASSOCIATION

When you are training a Recall, you want to build an association between the cue "Come" and a food reward, as this will motivate your puppy to come running every time you call. There is a very effective way of doing this if you invest in a whistle.

• Prepare your dog's food and ask him to "Sit". Blow twice on the whistle and then place the bowl on the floor. Repeat this procedure at every mealtime and your dog will learn that two toots on the whistle equals food.
• When your pup has a reliable Wait, you can ask him to "Sit" and "Wait", and then walk a few paces away with the food bowl. Blow twice on the whistle and call your pup to his bowl.
• If you have a helper, you can do a longer Recall, as the pup can

be held and then released when you blow the whistle. You can even ask your helper to hold the dog in an adjoining room and then blow the whistle. You will be amazed at the speed of your dog's Recall!

WORKING OUTSIDE

Once your dog has built up a good association with the whistle, you can practise the Recall in the garden. At this stage, you can introduce the clicker to mark the correct response.

• Take your dog outside and give him the chance to go off and explore.
• Wait until your dog has taken his focus away from you, and then blow twice on the whistle. When

Give your dog lots of encouragement as he comes towards you.

TRAINING TIP

Remember that your dog will be reading your body language and listening to your tone of voice when you are training the Recall. For this exercise, make yourself appear really exciting so that your dog wants to come to you. Use a higher tone of voice, open your arms out wide, and make a huge fuss of your dog when he comes to you.

your dog responds and comes to you, click, give lots of praise, and reward him with a treat. Let your dog go off and explore again.

- You can practise a couple of times, but do not let your dog go off the boil. You want him to

Reward your dog with a treat and lots of praise.

come powering towards you, full of enthusiasm.

- If your dog is more interested in toys, you can produce his favourite toy, and the reward will be coming to you for a game.

WORKING WITH DISTRACTIONS

When you are confident that your dog is responding to the Recall in the garden, it is time to introduce distractions. Initially, you can try a Recall when someone else is in the garden, or, if you have another dog, try a Recall when the two dogs are playing.

The next step is to venture into the outside world:

- Choose a place that is completely safe, such as a fenced recreation ground, so there is no danger from traffic.
- Let your dog off the lead, and once he has had a chance to run and explore, call him back to you using the whistle.
- When your dog responds, click, give him lots of praise and maybe a few bonus treats so that he knows he has been brilliant!

- Let your dog run free again before trying another Recall. It is very important that your dog sees the Recall as a fun exercise rather than a signal that his free run has come to an end.
- When your dog is responding well to the Recall in the safe, free-running area you have selected, you can be more ambitious and take him on some more exciting walks, such as in woods or to a park where he is likely to meet other dogs. By this stage, your dog should be happy to come to you in all situations.

OVERCOMING RECALL PROBLEMS

If you have worked at your Recall training from an early age, you should have built up a reliable response. However, there are times, particularly during adolescence, when a dog will test his boundaries, and this may result in a reluctance to come when called. Equally, you may have taken on an older, rescued dog that has had little in the way of positive training. In both situations, the best plan is to go back to basics and retrain the Recall so that you build up a good response. This is far more effective than shouting at your dog and getting no response, as this simply builds up a pattern in which your dog thinks it is OK to ignore you.

Try the following to improve your dog's Recall:

• Restrict your outings to safe, enclosed areas with minimal distractions so you can build up a better response. The more success you have (i.e. the more times your dog responds to the Recall), the more likely he is to keep coming to you. You are building up a cycle of desirable behaviour rather than allowing him to keep repeating the behaviour you do not want.

• Arm yourself with some special treats and use them only for

The aim is to build up a really enthusiastic response to the Recall.

TRAINING TIP

If you are going on a routine walk and your dog knows the route, he may decide that he will not respond to a Recall at the end of the walk, because he knows that this is where you clip on his lead. There are two ways to counteract this:

• Keep your dog guessing. Recall your dog at intervals throughout the walk and clip on his lead. Ask your dog to walk to Heel for a few paces and then release him. In this way, your dog sees Recall and walking to Heel as ways of interacting with you throughout the walk – not as the end of his fun.
• Take some really tasty treats with you, such as cheese or sausage, and reserve them for the final Recall at the end of the walk. This ups the reward, and should motivate your dog to come to you, even though he knows it is the end of his walk.

TRAINING TIP

If you are still experiencing difficulty with the Recall, you can use a training line, which will ensure success and will give you the opportunity to retrain your dog from scratch. A training line is the equivalent of a very long lead, which is specially designed to overcome training problems. It is 10 metres (33 feet) in length.

The purpose of the training line is to prevent your dog from disobeying you so that he never has the chance to get into bad habits. For example, when you call your dog and he ignores you, you can immediately pick up the end of the training line and call him again. By picking up the line you will have attracted his attention, and if you call in an excited, happy voice, he will come to you. The moment he comes to you, give him lots of praise and a tasty treat so he has an instant reward for making the 'right' decision. You will need to keep on using the training line over a period of time so you can reinforce the correct behaviour and build up a strong Recall.

The training line is also very useful if you have a dog that dodges out of the way just as you go to clip on his lead. If your dog is on a training line, you can tread on the line and halt his progress. You can then call him to you and reward him. Again, you will have to work at this for a number of training sessions, but every time he gets it right and is rewarded, he is more likely to repeat the behaviour you want.

A training line gives you control, so you can halt your dog's progress and then call him to you.

When you begin training the Recall, choose your moments wisely. If your dog is distracted his response will be poor.

Recalls. This should help to boost your dog's enthusiasm for coming back to you.

- If your dog is slow to respond, make yourself irresistible. Jump up or down, or try running off in the opposite direction. Your dog will think that you are having fun, so he will want to come and join in.

- Try calling your dog when you are out of his sight but you can still see him. This will take your dog out of his comfort zone, as he cannot see you. He will be slightly anxious and therefore more likely to respond to your whistle.

- Read the situation and only call your dog when you have a good chance of a positive response. For example, if your dog is playing with another dog – and has a history of poor Recalls – your chances of success are minimal. If you keep on calling and whistling, he will gain confidence because he knows where you are, and will continue playing with his new friend. In this instance, it is far better to go and get your dog rather than allow him to ignore you.

FORMAL RECALL

If your dog is progressing well with his training, you may want to try a formal Recall, which is used in Competitive Obedience competitions. This involves putting together a number of elements to produce the complete exercise.

- Stand with your dog on your left-hand side and ask him to "Sit".

- Give the verbal cue "Wait" and walk away from your dog, moving off on your right foot, which is furthest from the dog's side.

- Walk away and halt when you are approximately five metres (15 ft) from your dog.

- Turn and face your dog, repeating the command "Wait".

- Call your dog, opening your arms out and then closing your hands together as your dog comes in to you. This gives your dog a marker to aim for.

- Tell your dog to "Sit" as he comes to you.

You can finish the exercise here, or, if you want to be really flashy, you can teach him to "Finish" so that he returns to your left-hand side and goes into the Sit.

FORMAL RECALL

Start with your dog on your left-hand side and ask him to "Wait".

Leave your dog.

Call your dog.

Give lots of praise as your dog comes in to you.

Walk a distance from your dog before turning to face him.

This is the 'Present' position.

The exercise is finished when the dog returns to the handler's left-hand side.

TEACHING A FINISH

There are two ways of doing a Finish: the dog can go around the back of your legs to return to your left-hand side, or he can walk forwards, turn alongside you, and then Sit at your left-hand side. This is known as the Continental Finish.

- To teach your dog to go around the back of your legs, it is easiest to use a treat to lure him into position, clicking when he achieves the correct position.
- If he is struggling, click when he is halfway round, and repeat the exercise, gradually building it up, stage by stage, until he is in the correct position.
- If you are teaching the Continental Finish, work with your dog on the lead, and step back with your left foot, guiding your dog to come in close to you. When he is in the correct position, click and reward.
- Keep practising, working in stages if necessary, until your dog will understand what is required. Do not introduce the verbal cue "Finish" until your dog fully understands the exercise.

INSTANT DOWN

This may sound like a stationary exercise, but the aim is to train your dog to go into a Down regardless of what he is doing. He may be standing still, walking away from you, or running at full tilt in the opposite direction. This can be used as a simple means of control, so you can get your dog's attention, or it could be a lifesaver

To begin with, your dog will respond to the hand signal, but in time he should react instantly to the verbal cue.

if your dog is running towards a busy road.

In essence, an Instant Down is a nothing more than a speedy response to the Down cue that you have already taught (see page 98). However, for this exercise your dog needs to respond instantly to the verbal cue 'Down', with no hesitation and no need for hand signals.

- Start working with your dog on-lead so you have control. Initially, practise Down at your left-hand side, using a hand signal if required.

- Now use a verbal cue and drop the hand signal. Your dog may need a moment to think, particularly if he has become dependent on the hand signal, so be patient. The beauty of clicker training is that you can afford to wait; your dog knows he has to come up with something to earn a click. If you have trained him stage by stage, he should be able to respond to the verbal cue without further assistance.
- The moment your dog goes into a Down, click and make a big

103

TRAINING TIP

The aim is to get an instant response, so work at your tone of voice when you are giving the cue. You need to sound very firm and give a feeling of urgency so your dog drops into position without hesitating. Remember, in this instance you are not asking your dog, you are telling him. It could be the difference between life and death.

- When your dog is going into a Down on the move, you can unclip his lead and practise a lead-free Down. By this stage, your dog should understand the exercise, and being off-lead should not cause problems.

- Now leave your dog in a Sit or a Stand, and walk away from him. Then give the verbal cue "Down". Your dog should be fully attuned to the cue, and he should respond, even though you are not standing next to him.

- Keep working on this, standing at some distance in front and to the side, so your dog is no longer concerned where you are standing.

- Finally, try standing behind your dog when he is sitting or standing and give the cue. This is the big test, as your dog must respond to your voice, even though you are not in his sight. This may take a bit of practice, so make a real fuss of your dog when he gets it right.

- You are now ready to try the Instant Down where your dog is off lead and has not been put in a Sit or a Stand. Start working at this in the garden where there will be fewer distractions, and then test it in a number of different environments, always giving lots of praise and high-value rewards so your dog develops a fast and reliable response in all situations.

fuss of him, maybe adding a few bonus treats. Keep practising until your dog is responding immediately to the verbal cue.

- Now try walking with your dog at your side, halting and giving the Down cue. Again, your dog may be slow to begin with, as you have changed the exercise, but he will soon get the idea.

- Next, run with your dog and then give the cue "Down". Your dog may get a bit over-excited, working at a faster pace, but persevere until he gives the correct response.

RETRIEVE

This is not an essential exercise to teach your dog, but it builds up the rapport between you and can be the basis of providing physical exercise combined with mental stimulation, which all dogs need.

The Retrieve is another exercise with several elements that need to be taught individually before they are linked together. Paradoxically, the elements are taught in pretty much the reverse order of the sequence you are aiming to put together. This is to keep each lesson separate in the dog's mind so that he does not become confused.

HOLD

The first step is to get your dog interested in the toy you want him to fetch. To start with, choose a toy your dog likes to hold – it could be a soft toy, a tennis ball, or a rubber hoop. At this stage, you want to motivate your dog, so make it as easy for him as you can.

- Kneel on the floor next to your dog and show him the toy. If you have a toy-mad dog, he will focus on it immediately and try to get at it. If your dog is not so keen, play a game with the toy,

The first step is to teach your dog to hold his toy.

TRAINING TIP

If your dog is reluctant to hold his toy, build up the exercise in stages. The clicker allows you to reward small steps of progress, which helps to keep your dog motivated as well as helping you to achieve your goal. So click and reward your dog if he comes up and sniffs the toy, then when he opens his mouth and holds it for a split second, then when he holds the toy independently. Do not get frustrated; celebrate your dog's success, even though it may be minimal, and you will find that your dog will gradually get focused on his toy.

- When your dog is taking the toy from your hand on the verbal cue "Hold", increase the difficulty and ask him to Hold when the toy is on the ground. This may take some time, as the toy has become a passive object and does not offer the stimulation of a toy held in the hand that you can move around.

- If your dog is slow to hold his toy, try to get him interested by moving the toy around when it is on the floor. Click and reward when your dog attempts to get the toy, and then try again when the toy is motionless. Be lavish with your praise when your dog gets it right.

Be ready to reward small steps of progress. This dog is learning to hold a dumbbell.

The dog must be willing to give up his dumbbell on request.

dragging it across the floor, throwing it up and catching it, and hiding it behind your back. This should spark his interest.

- Now give the toy to your dog. Be ready with the clicker, and click as soon as he holds the toy. Be careful with your timing; the click must come when the toy is in his mouth – not as he spits it out.
- Keep practising, waiting a few seconds longer before you click, so your dog gets used to the toy being in his mouth.
- If you have a super-keen dog that wants to hold the toy and then run off with it, keep your dog on lead while you practise so you retain control.
- When your dog is happy to hold his toy, introduce the verbal cue "Hold", then click and reward.

GIVE

When your dog is happy to hold his toy, he needs to learn to give it to you.

- Give the cue "Hold", and then call your dog to you. Wait a few seconds, and then take the toy from his mouth. Click and reward. Do not snatch or grab, as your dog will think this is part of the game and will try to make off with his trophy.
- If your dog is reluctant to give up his toy, show him that you have a treat, or exchange toys so that your dog does not think he is giving up his prized possession.
- Keep practising, and when your dog is giving his toy willingly, introduce the cue "Give".

COME

The aim is for the dog to come to you, holding the toy, and then give it to you. Asking the dog to "Come" rather than following his desire to run off with the toy can be tricky, so it is best to teach the "Come" element before your dog has the added stimulation of seeing the toy being thrown.

- Ask your dog to "Hold" his toy, and back off a few paces.
- Now ask him to "Come". When he responds, give him lots of praise, stroking him and letting him hold on to the toy before you ask him to "Give". In this way your dog learns to Hold the toy for a little longer rather than spit it out as soon as he gets to you. If he is keen on hanging on to his toy, stroking and praising him will encourage him to relax and to enjoy interacting with you.
- After a few moments, give the cue "Hold", and when your dog gives up his toy, click and reward.
- Keep practising, backing away a little further each time, so your dog gets used to coming towards you with his toy in his mouth.

FETCH

Now you want your dog to run out and "Fetch" his toy. If you have one of the retriever breeds, such as a Labrador or a Golden Retriever, which have been specifically bred to retrieve, your dog will be only too happy to oblige. Other breeds do not have such instinctive behaviour, but most will respond to a moving object, and, with practice, will

Encourage the dog to come towards you, holding his dumbbell.

You need to encourage your dog to run out and "Fetch".

FORMAL RETRIEVE

The dog must "Wait" at the handler's side while the toy is thrown.

The dog goes out to "Fetch" the toy.

A clean pick-up.

The dog returns to the handler and presents the toy.

The handler takes the toy.

The exercise is finished when the dog returns to the handler's left-hand side.

understand what is required.

- Start off by showing your dog the toy and getting him interested in it.
- When he is focused on the toy, throw it, and, as he approaches the toy, give the cue "Hold".
- At this stage, it is best to approach your dog so he only has to "Come" a few paces before you ask him to "Give" the toy.
- Keep working on this, and when your dog is running out smartly as soon as you have thrown the toy, introduce the verbal cue "Fetch".

You now have a dog that will run out to fetch his toy, hold it and bring it back to you. This is the basis for lots of fun games, which you will both thoroughly enjoy.

If you are feeling ambitious, and your dog is enjoying his training, you may want to increase the degree of difficulty so he can do a Formal Retrieve, which is one of the exercises performed in Competitive Obedience.

FORMAL RETRIEVE

The major difference between a Formal Retrieve and a Play Retrieve is that the dog must "Wait" until his toy is thrown before he is given the cue to "Fetch". Basically, all you need to do is to work at your "Wait" so that your dog stays in place despite the stimulation of seeing the toy being thrown. The dog must also sit to present the toy, which needs a little more discipline.

The Formal Retrieve involves the following steps:

- Position your dog at your left-hand side and ask him to "Sit".
- When you have his attention, ask him to "Wait" and then throw his toy.
- The dog must remain motionless at your side until you ask him to "Fetch". This cue should be given after the toy has landed.
- When the dog is running out towards the toy, give the cue "Hold".
- By this stage of training, the dog should know that he needs to head towards you, but back him up with the cue to "Come".
- When your dog comes in front of you, ask him to "Sit".
- Wait a few moments, and then ask him to "Give".
- The exercise is completed by asking your dog to "Finish" so he returns to his starting position at your left-hand side.

When your dog has become a polished retriever, you can vary the toys or articles he retrieves. In Competitive Obedience, the dog will start off working with a dumbbell, and then, in the more advanced

In advanced classes the judge will choose the retrieve article.

classes, he must retrieve an article of the judge's choice. This can be big or small, soft or hard, so the dog has to learn to pick up and hold a variety of objects that have different textures.

This can also be useful at home if you train your dog to pick up different items, such as keys or the TV remote, on cue.

PROBLEM BEHAVIOUR

Chapter 11

I f you have trained your dog from puppyhood, survived his adolescence and established yourself as a fair and consistent leader, you will end up with a brilliant companion dog. However, problems may arise unexpectedly, or you may have taken on a rescued dog that has established behavioural problems. If you are worried about your dog and feel out of your depth, do not delay in seeking professional help. This is readily available, usually through a referral from your vet, or you can find out additional information on the internet (see Appendices for web addresses). An animal behaviourist will have experience in tackling problem behaviour and will be able to help both you and your dog.

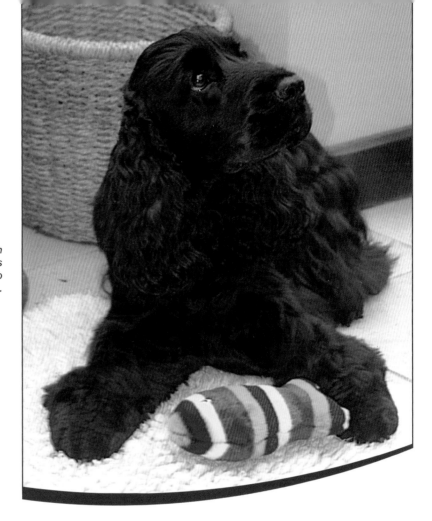

A dog with an elevated status may attempt to guard his toys.

ASSERTIVE BEHAVIOUR

If you have trained and socialised your dog correctly, he will know his place in the family pack and will have no desire to challenge your authority. Adolescent dogs may test the boundaries, so this is the time to enforce all your earlier training so your dog accepts his place in the family. However, it may be that you have a overly assertive dog who continually tries his luck, or you may have taken on a rescued dog that has not been properly trained or socialised.

Assertive behaviour is expressed in different forms, but by far the most common is resource guarding. A dog has something he wants – it could be a toy, his food bowl, his bed – and he has no intention of giving it up. He may also seek to improve his status by deciding he wants your place on the sofa, and once he is there, he refuses to budge. He will give a warning growl, which means: "Don't come any closer – this is mine".

In both situations, the dog is 'guarding' something he values, but, more importantly, he is showing lack of respect for you. If you see signs of your dog resource guarding, you must work at refocusing his attention. Although you need to be firm, you also need to use positive training methods so that your dog is rewarded for the behaviour you want. In this way, his 'correct' behaviour will be strengthened and repeated.

There are a number of steps you can take to lower your dog's status and put a stop to resource guarding. They include:

• If your dog has been guarding his food bowl, put the bowl down

Your dog should be willing to give up possessions on request, even if it is a high-value treat, such as a bone.

empty and drop in a little food at a time. Periodically stop dropping in the food, and tell your dog to "Sit" and "Wait". Give it a few seconds, and then reward him by dropping in more food. This shows your dog that you are the provider of the food and he can only eat when you allow him to.

- Make sure the family eats before you feed your dog. Some trainers advocate eating in front of the dog (maybe just a few bites from a biscuit) before starting a training session.

- If your dog has taken to sitting on the sofa or growling when you approach his bed, do not be confrontational – this will only make matters worse. Attract your dog with a toy or a treat so that he makes the decision to jump off the sofa or leave his bed. Then, ask him to do something positive, such as a Sit or a Down, or retrieving his toy. This will give you the chance to reward 'good' behaviour. Keep repeating this and you will break the impasse. Your dog has

voluntarily changed his mindset, and this gives you the opportunity to show your leadership in a positive light.

- Follow the same procedure outlined above if your dog is becoming possessive over a toy. Do not confront him and force him to give up the toy, as this will only exacerbate the situation. Organise a swap so your dog is willing to give up his toy – and then follow it up with some positive training.

- Do not let your dog barge through doors ahead of you or leap from the back of the car before you release him. You may not think this is important – but it is as far as your dog is concerned because he is following his own agenda without reference to you. Every time you get your dog out of the car, ask him to "Wait", clip on his lead, and then allow him to jump out. You can underline this training, if necessary, by teaching your dog to "Wait" at doorways, and then rewarding him for letting you go through first.

- Go back to basics and hold daily training sessions. Make sure you have some really tasty treats, or find a toy your dog really values and only bring it out at training sessions. Run through all the training exercises you have taught your dog. Make a big fuss of him and reward him when he does well. This will reinforce the message that you are the leader because you 'own' high-value rewards, and he needs to co-operate with you to earn them.

- Teach your dog something new. This can be as simple as learning a trick, such as shaking paws. Having something new to think about will mentally stimulate your dog, and he will benefit from interacting with you.

If your dog is progressing well with his retraining programme, think about getting involved with a dog sport, such as Agility or Competitive Obedience. This will give your dog a positive outlet for his energies. However, if your dog is still seeking to be assertive, or you have any other concerns, do not delay in seeking the help of an animal behaviourist.

ATTENTION SEEKING

This type of behaviour is expressed in different ways, but the most common are jumping up, barking and whining. This may be the result of a dog that has been poorly trained and does not understand appropriate behaviour, it may be because the dog is anxious, or it may be that the dog is being pushy because he is seeking to elevate his status.

In all situations, the key is to ignore your dog (see Chapter Three, page 43). If a dog craves attention, he will not care what form it comes in. If he barks and you shout at him, telling him to be quiet, that is rewarding. If he jumps up and you push him down, that, too, is rewarding. However, if you ignore him, he will

realise that his attention-seeking behaviour is non-productive.

Try the following:

- When your dog jumps up, turn your back on him and remain motionless until your dog stops trying to jump up. Do not say anything and do not be tempted to turn round until he is standing quietly.
- The moment your dog has given up his attention-seeking behaviour, reward him with your attention. Ask him to do

something simple, such as Sit or a Down, and then make a huge fuss of him.

- If your dog is barking, adopt a similar procedure as outlined above. Most importantly, do not give him eye contact, as this will encourage him to keep going.
- Be consistent in ignoring attention-seeking behaviour, but equally, make sure you spend quality time with your dog. This will give him the attention he wants – but on your terms.

Attention-seeking behaviour must be nipped in the bud.

SEPARATION ANXIETY

It is important that your dog learns to accept short periods of separation without becoming anxious. A new puppy should be left for short periods on his own, ideally in a crate where he cannot get up to any mischief. It is a good idea to leave him with a boredom-busting toy (see page 66) so he will be happily occupied in your absence. When you return, do not rush to the crate and make a huge fuss. Wait a few minutes, and then calmly go to the crate and release your dog, telling him how good he has been. If this scenario is repeated a number of times, your dog will soon learn that being left on his own is no big deal. As your dog grows up, keep to the routine of making minimum fuss when you leave the house and ignoring your dog for a few minutes when you return. In this way, your dog learns to accept comings and goings as a matter of course.

Problems with separation anxiety are most likely to arise if you take on a rescued dog that has major insecurities. You may also find that your dog hates being left if you have failed to accustom him to short periods of isolation when he was growing up. Separation anxiety is expressed in a number of ways, and all are equally distressing for both dog and owner. An anxious dog that is left alone may bark and whine continuously, urinate and defecate, and may be extremely destructive.

There are a number of steps you can take when attempting to solve this problem.

Your dog must learn to accept your absences without becoming anxious.

- Put up a baby-gate between adjoining rooms, and leave your dog in one room while you are in the other room. Your dog will be able to see you and hear you, but he is learning to cope without being right next to you. Build up the amount of time you can leave your dog in easy stages.
- Buy some boredom-busting toys and fill them with tasty treats. Whenever you leave your dog, give him a food-filled toy so that he is busy while you are away.
- If you have not used a crate before, it is not too late to start. Make sure the crate is big and comfortable, and train your dog to get used to going in his crate while you are in the same room. Gradually build up the amount of time he spends in the crate, and then start leaving the room for short periods. When you return, do not make a fuss of your dog. Leave him for five or 10 minutes before releasing him so that he

gets used to your comings and goings.

- Pretend to go out, putting on your coat and jangling your keys, but do not leave the house. An anxious dog often becomes hyped up by the ritual of leave taking, and so this will help to desensitise him.
- When you go out, leave a radio or a TV on. Some dogs are comforted by hearing voices and background noise when they are left alone.
- You can train your dog to understand a signal so that he knows that you are going out, but you will be returning. For example, put a can of baked beans on the kitchen counter, making sure your dog sees what you are doing. Leave the room, return in a few minutes and put the can back in the cupboard. Build this up over a period of time, making your absences longer, and your dog will learn to 'read' the signal and will remain calm and settled until you return.
- Try to make your absences as short as possible when you are first training your dog to accept being on his own. When you return, leave him for a few minutes, and when you go to him remain calm and relaxed so that he does not become hyped up with a huge greeting.

If you take these steps, your dog should become less anxious, and, over a period of time, you should be able to solve the problem. However,

if you are failing to make progress, do not delay in call in expert help.

AGGRESSION

Aggression is a complex issue, as there are different causes and the behaviour may be triggered by numerous factors. It may directed towards people, but more commonly it is directec towards other dogs. Aggressi dogs may be the result of:

- Dominance (see page 14?
- Defensive behaviour: This be induced by fear, pain o punishment.
- Territory: A dog may becor aggressive if strange dogs or people enter his territory (which is generally seen as the house and garden).
- Intra-sexual issues: This is aggression between sexes male-to-male or female-to-female.
- Parental instinct: A bitch may become aggressive if she is protecting her puppies.

A dog who has been well socialised (see Chapter Five) and has been given sufficient exposure to other dogs at significant stages of his development will rarely be aggressive. In fact, a dog that has been reared correctly should not have a hint of aggression in his temperament. Obviously, if you have taken on an older, rescued dog, you will have little or no knowledge of

If your dog is unreliable with other dogs, it is advisable to use a safety muzzle as this often has a calming effect. However, if you are worried about your dog's behaviour, you should seek expert advice.

his background, and if he shows signs of aggression, the cause will need to be determined. In most cases, you would be well advised to call in professional help if you see aggressive behaviour in your dog. If the aggression is directed towards people, you should seek immediate advice. This behaviour can escalate very quickly and could have disastrous consequences.

NEW CHALLENGES

Chapter 12

I f you enjoy training your dog, you may want to try one of the many programmes, activities or dog sports that are now on offer.

GOOD CITIZEN SCHEME

This is a scheme run by the Kennel Club in the UK. It promotes responsible ownership and helps you to train a well-behaved dog who will fit in with the community. The schemes are excellent for all pet owners, and they are also a good starting point if you plan to compete with your dog when he is older. There are three levels: bronze, silver and gold, with each test becoming progressively more demanding.

Some of the exercises include:
• Walking on a loose lead among people and other dogs.
• Recall amid distractions.
• A controlled greeting where

dogs stay under control while owners meet.

- The dog allows all-over grooming and handling by its owner, and also accepts being handled by the examiner.
- Stays, with the owner in sight, and then out of sight.
- Food manners, allowing the owner to eat without begging, and taking a treat on command.
- Sendaway – sending the dog to his bed.

The tests are designed to show the control you have over your dog, and his ability to respond correctly and remain calm in all situations. The Good Citizen Scheme is taught at most training clubs. For more information, log on to the Kennel Club website (see Appendices).

SHOWING

If you have a pedigree dog, you may want to get involved in the world of showing. This is a highly competitive sport, particularly in popular breeds, such as Labrador Retrievers, West Highland White Terriers, and Cocker Spaniels, which attract huge entries. However, many owners get bitten by the showing bug, and their calendar is governed by the dates of the top showing fixtures.

To be successful in the show ring, your dog must conform as closely as possible to the Breed Standard, which is a written blueprint describing the 'perfect' specimen of the breed. To get started you need

A controlled greeting is one of the exercises in Good Citizen tests.

Do you fancy the challenge of exhibiting your dog in the show ring?

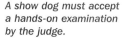

A show dog must accept a hands-on examination by the judge.

to buy a puppy that has show potential and then train him to perform in the ring. A dog will be expected to stand in show pose, gait for the judge in order to show off his natural movement, and to be examined by the judge. This involves a detailed hands-on examination, so your dog must be bombproof when handled by strangers.

Many training clubs hold ringcraft classes, which are run by experienced showgoers. At these classes, you will learn how to handle your dog in the ring, and you will also find out about rules, procedures and show ring etiquette.

Start off at small, informal shows where you can practise and learn the tricks of the trade before graduating to bigger shows. It's a long haul starting in the very first puppy class, but the dream is to make your dog up into a breed Champion.

COMPETITIVE OBEDIENCE

Border Collies, Working Sheepdogs and German Shepherds dominate this sport, but other breeds have also made their mark, so why not have a go? The challenge of Competitive Obedience is not only teaching the individual exercises, but also performing them with the accuracy and precision that is demanded. The classes become progressively more difficult with additional exercises and the handler giving minimal instructions to the dog.

Exercises include:

• **Heelwork:** Dog and handler

This highly trained dog has picked out the correct cloth in a scent discrimination test.

must complete a set pattern on and off the lead, which includes left turns, right turns, about turns, and changes of pace.

- **Recall:** This may be when the handler is stationary or on the move.
- **Retrieve:** This may be a dumbbell or any article chosen by the judge.
- **Sendaway:** The dog is sent to a designated spot and must go into an instant Down until he is recalled by the handler.
- **Stays:** The dog must stay in the Sit and in the Down for a set amount of time. In advanced classes, the handler is out of sight.
- **Scent:** The dog must retrieve a single cloth from a pre-arranged pattern of cloths that has his owner's scent, or, in advanced classes, the judge's scent. There may also be decoy cloths.
- **Distance control:** The dog must execute a series of moves (Sit, Stand, Down) without moving from his position and with the handler at a distance.

Even though Competitive Obedience requires a high measure of control, make it fun for your dog, with lots of praise and rewards so that you motivate him to do his best. Many training clubs run advanced classes for those who want to compete in obedience, or you can hire the services of a professional trainer for one-on-one sessions.

AGILITY

This fun sport has grown enormously in popularity over the past few years. It is open to all breeds as well as crossbreeds and mongrels. The classes are simply divided into sizes: Small, Medium and Large, and the equipment is modified accordingly.

If you fancy having a go, make sure you have good control over your dog and keep him slim. Agility is a very physical sport, which demands fitness from both dog and handler. A fat dog is never going to make it as an Agility competitor.

In Agility competitions, each dog must complete a set course over a series of obstacles, which include:
- Jumps (upright hurdles and long jump)

All types of dog can compete in Agility as classes are divided by size.

Gundog breeds showcase their natural working ability in Field Trials.

- Weaves
- A-frame
- Dog walk
- Seesaw
- Tunnels (collapsible and rigid)
- Tyre

Dogs may compete in Jumping classes with jumps, tunnels and weaves, or in Agility classes, which have the full set of equipment. Faults are awarded for poles down on the jumps, missed contact points on the A-frame, dog walk and seesaw, and refusals. If a dog takes the wrong course, he is eliminated. The winner is the dog that completes the course in the fastest time with no faults. As you progress up the grades, courses become progressively harder with more twists, turns and changes of direction.

If you want to bcome involved in Agility, you will need to find a club that specialises in the sport (see Appendices).

Be aware that you will not be allowed to start training until your dog is 12 months old, and you cannot compete until he is 18 months old. This rule is for the protection of the dog, who may suffer injury if he puts strain on bones and joints while he is still growing.

FIELD TRIALS

This is a sport in which gundogs are tested on their natural working ability. Many gundogs are trained for a day's shooting, but if you want your dog to compete in Field Trials, he must perform the required exercises at the highest level.

In Field Trials, dogs are trained to work in an entirely natural environment. Nothing is set up, staged or artificial. The dogs may be asked to retrieve shot game from any type of terrain, including swamp, thick undergrowth and from water. They also need to perform blind retrieves, where they are sent out to find shot game when they haven't seen it fall. Dogs are judged on their natural game-finding abilities, their work in the shooting field, and their response to their handler. The two most crucial elements are steadiness and obedience. The goal is to make your dog into a Field Trial Champion.

The scale is a challenging obstacle to negotiate.

Tracking is one of the elements of Working Trials.

WORKING TRIALS

This is a very challenging sport, which has been adapted so that smaller breeds can take part as well as the bigger breeds, such as Rottweilers, German Shepherd Dogs and Border Collies, which traditionally excel at Working Trials. The sport consists of three basic components:

- **Control:** Dog and handler must complete obedience exercises, but the work does not have to be as precise as it is in Competitive Obedience. In the advanced classes, manwork (where the dog works as a guard/protection dog) is a major feature.
- **Agility:** The dog must negotiate a hurdle, a long jump, and an

Flyball is fast and furious – and dogs love it!

upright scale, which is the most taxing piece of dog equipment.

- **Nosework:** The dog must follow a track that has been laid over a set course. The surface may vary, and the length of time between the track being laid and the dog starting work is increased in the advanced classes.

The ladder of stakes are: Companion Dog, Utility Dog, Working Dog, Tracking Dog and Patrol Dog.

If you want to get involved in Working Trials, you will need to find a specialist club or a trainer that specialises in the sport. For more information, see Appendices.

FLYBALL

Flyball is a team sport. The dogs love it, and it is undoubtedly the noisiest of all the canine sports!

Four dogs are selected to run in a relay race against an opposing team. The dogs are sent out by their handlers to jump four hurdles, catch the ball from the Flyball box, and then return over the hurdles. At the top level, this sport is fast and furious, and although it is dominated by Border Collies and Working Sheepdogs, other breeds, and crossbreeds, can compete with great success. This is particularly true in multi-breed competitions where the team is made up of four dogs of different breeds, and only one can be a Border Collie or a Working Sheepdog.

DANCING WITH DOGS

This sport is relatively new, but it is becoming increasingly popular. It is very entertaining to watch, but it is certainly not as simple as it looks. To perform a choreographed routine to music with your dog demands a huge amount of training.

Dancing with dogs is divided into

It takes a lot of work to build up a repertoire of moves and tricks and then create a dancing routine with your dog.

two categories: Heelwork to Music and Canine Freestyle. In Heelwork to Music, the dog must work closely with his handler and show a variety of close 'heelwork' positions. In Canine Freestyle, the routine can be more flamboyant, with the dog working at a distance from the handler and performing spectacular tricks. Routines are judged on style and presentation, content and accuracy.

SUMMING UP

You may have ambitions to be a top competitor, or you may be content to train your dog so that he is an outstanding family companion. Regardless of your goal, give your dog the quality time and commitment he deserves. The 'perfect' dog does not come ready-made. He needs guidance and leadership so that he understands his place in the family circle – and in the community. Make sure you keep your half of the bargain – training and socialising your dog – and you will be rewarded with companionship that is second to none.

USEFUL ADDRESSES

KENNEL CLUBS

UK
The Kennel Club
1-5 Clarges Street, London, W1J 8AB
Tel: 0870 606 6750
Fax: 0207 518 1058
Web: www.the-kennel-club.org.uk

USA
American Kennel Club (AKC)
5580 Centerview Drive,
Raleigh, NC 27606, USA.
Tel: 919 233 9767
Fax: 919 233 3627
Email: info@akc.org
Web: www.akc.org

United Kennel Club (UKC)
100 E Kilgore Rd, Kalamazoo,
MI 49002-5584, USA.
Tel: 269 343 9020
Fax: 269 343 7037
Web:www.ukcdogs.com/

AUSTRALIA
Australian National Kennel Council (ANKC)
The Australian National Kennel Council is the administrative body for pure breed canine affairs in Australia. It does not, however, deal directly with dog exhibitors, breeders or judges. For information pertaining to breeders, clubs or shows, please contact the relevant State or Territory Controlling Body.

Dogs Australian Capital Teritory
PO Box 815, Dickson ACT 2602
Tel: (02) 6241 4404
Fax: (02) 6241 1129
Email: administrator@dogsact.org.au
Web: www.dogsact.org.au

Dogs New South Wales
PO Box 632, St Marys, NSW 1790
Tel: (02) 9834 3022 or 1300 728 022 (NSW Only)
Fax: (02) 9834 3872
Email: info@dogsnsw.org.au
Web: www.dogsnsw.org.au

Dogs Northern Territory
PO Box 37521, Winnellie NT 0821
Tel: (08) 8984 3570
Fax: (08) 8984 3409
Email: admin@dogsnt.com.au
Web: www.dogsnt.com.au

Dogs Queensland
PO Box 495, Fortitude Valley Qld 4006
Tel: (07) 3252 2661
Fax: (07) 3252 3864
Email: info@dogsqueensland.org.au
Web: www.dogsqueensland.org.au

Dogs South Australia
PO Box 844
Prospect East SA 5082
Tel: (08) 8349 4797
Fax: (08) 8262 5751
Email: info@dogssa.com.au
Web: www.dogssa.com.au

Tasmanian Canine Association Inc
The Rothman Building
PO Box 116
Glenorchy Tas 7010
Tel: (03) 6272 9443
Fax: (03) 6273 0844
Email: tca@iprimus.com.au
Web: www.tasdogs.com

Dogs Victoria
Locked Bag K9
Cranbourne VIC 3977
Tel: (03)9788 2500
Fax: (03) 9788 2599
Email: office@dogsvictoria.org.au
Web: www.dogsvictoria.org.au

Dogs Western Australia
PO Box 1404, Canning Vale WA 6970
Tel: (08) 9455 1188
Fax: (08) 9455 1190
Email: k9@dogswest.com
Web: www.dogswest.com

INTERNATIONAL
Fédération Cynologique Internationalé (FCI)/World Canine Organisation
Place Albert 1er, 13, B-6530 Thuin,
Belgium.
Tel: +32 71 59.12.38
Fax: +32 71 59.22.29
Web: www.fci.be/

TRAINING AND BEHAVIOUR

UK
Association of Pet Dog Trainers
PO Box 17, Kempsford, GL7 4WZ
Telephone: 01285 810811
Email: APDToffice@aol.com
Web: http://www.apdt.co.uk

Association of Pet Behaviour Counsellors
PO BOX 46, Worcester, WR8 9YS
Telephone: 01386 751151
Fax: 01386 750743
Email: info@apbc.org.uk
Web: http://www.apbc.org.uk/

USA
Association of Pet Dog Trainers
101 North Main Street, Suite 610
Greenville, SC 29601, USA.
Tel: 1 800 738 3647
Email: information@apdt.com
Web: www.apdt.com/

American College of Veterinary Behaviorists
College of Veterinary Medicine, 4474 Tamu,
Texas A&M University
College Station, Texas 77843-4474
Web: http://dacvb.org/

American Veterinary Society of Animal Behavior
Web: www.avsabonline.org/

AUSTRALIA
APDT Australia Inc
PO Box 3122, Bankstown Square, NSW 2200,
Email: secretary@apdt.com.au
Web: www.apdt.com.au

Canine Behaviour
For details of regional behvaiourists, contact the relevant State or Territory Controlling Body.

ACTIVITIES

UK
Agility Club
http://www.agilityclub.co.uk/

British Flyball Association
PO Box 990, Doncaster, DN1 9FY
Telephone: 01628 829623
Email: secretary@flyball.org.uk
Web: http://www.flyball.org.uk/

USA
North American Dog Agility Council
P.O. Box 1206, Colbert,
OK 74733, USA.
Web: www.nadac.com/

North American Flyball Association, Inc.
1333 West Devon Avenue, #512
Chicago, IL 60660
Tel/Fax: 800 318 6312
Email: flyball@flyball.org
Web: www.flyball.org/

AUSTRALIA
Agility Dog Association of Australia
ADAA Secretary, PO Box 2212,
Gailes, QLD 4300, Australia.
Tel: 0423 138 914
Email: admin@adaa.com.au
Web: www.adaa.com.au/

NADAC Australia (North American Dog Agility Council - Australian Division)
12 Wellman Street, Box Hill South, Victoria 3128, Australia.
Email: shirlene@nadacaustralia.com
Web: www.nadacaustralia.com/

Australian Flyball Association
PO Box 4179, Pitt Town, NSW 2756
Tel: 0407 337 939
Email: info@flyball.org.au
Web: www.flyball.org.au/

INTERNATIONAL
World Canine Freestyle Organisation
P.O. Box 350122, Brooklyn, NY 11235-2525, USA
Tel: (718) 332-8336
Fax: (718) 646-2686
Email: wcfodogs@aol.com
Web: www.worldcaninefreestyle.org

HEALTH

UK
Alternative Veterinary Medicine Centre
Chinham House, Stanford in the Vale,
Oxfordshire, SN7 8NQ
Tel: 01367 710324
Fax: 01367 718243
Web: www.alternativevet.org/

British Small Animal Veterinary Association
Woodrow House, 1 Telford Way,
Waterwells Business Park, Quedgeley,
Gloucestershire, GL2 2AB
Tel: 01452 726700
Fax: 01452 726701
Email: customerservices@bsava.com
Web: http://www.bsava.com/

Royal College of Veterinary Surgeons
Belgravia House, 62-64 Horseferry Road,
London, SW1P 2AF
Tel: 0207 222 2001
Fax: 0207 222 2004
Email: admin@rcvs.org.uk
Web: www.rcvs.org.uk

USA
American Holistic Veterinary Medical Association
2218 Old Emmorton Road
Bel Air, MD 21015
Tel: 410 569 0795
Fax 410 569 2346
Email: office@ahvma.org
Web: www.ahvma.org/

American Veterinary Medical Association
1931 North Meacham Road, Suite 100,
Schaumburg, IL 60173-4360, USA.
Tel: 800 248 2862
Fax: 847 925 1329
Web: www.avma.org

American College of Veterinary Surgeons
19785 Crystal Rock Dr, Suite 305
Germantown, MD 20874, USA.
Tel: 301 916 0200
Toll Free: 877 217 2287
Fax: 301 916 2287
Email: acvs@acvs.org
Web: www.acvs.org/

AUSTRALIA
Australian Holistic Vets
Web: www.ahv.com.au/

Australian Small Animal Veterinary Association
40/6 Herbert Street, St Leonards, NSW 2065, Australia.
Tel: 02 9431 5090
Fax: 02 9437 9068
Email: asava@ava.com.au
Web: www.asava.com.au

Australian Veterinary Association
Unit 40, 6 Herbert Street, St Leonards, NSW 2065, Australia.
Tel: 02 9431 5000
Fax: 02 9437 9068
Web: www.ava.com.au

Australian College Veterinary Scientists
Building 3, Garden City Office Park,
2404 Logan Road, Eight Mile Plains,
Queensland 4113, Australia.
Tel: 07 3423 2016
Fax: 07 3423 2977
Email: admin@acvs.org.au
Web: http://acvsc.org.au

ASSISTANCE DOGS

UK
Canine Partners
Mill Lane, Heyshott,
Midhurst, GU29 0ED
Tel: 08456 580480
Fax: 08456 580481
Web: www.caninepartners.co.uk

Dogs for the Disabled
The Frances Hay Centre, Blacklocks Hill,
Banbury, Oxon, OX17 2BS
Tel: 01295 252600
Web: www.dogsforthedisabled.org

Guide Dogs for the Blind Association
Burghfield Common, Reading, RG7 3YG
Tel: 01189 835555
Fax: 01189 835433
Web: www.guidedogs.org.uk/

Hearing Dogs for Deaf People
The Grange, Wycombe Road, Saunderton,
Princes Risborough, Bucks, HP27 9NS
Tel: 01844 348100
Fax: 01844 348101
Web: www.hearingdogs.org.uk

Pets as Therapy
14a High Street, Wendover, Aylesbury, Bucks.
HP22 6EA.
Tel: 01845 345445
Fax: 01845 550236
Web: http://www.petsastherapy.org/

Support Dogs
21 Jessops Riverside, Brightside Lane,
Sheffield, S9 2RX
Tel: 01142 617800
Fax: 01142 617555
Email: supportdogs@btconnect.com
Web: www.support-dogs.org.uk

USA
Therapy Dogs International
88 Bartley Road, Flanders, NJ 07836,.
Tel: 973 252 9800
Fax: 973 252 7171
Web: www.tdi-dog.o

Therapy Dogs Inc.
P.O. Box 20227, Cheyenne, WY 82003.
Tel: 307 432 0272.
Fax: 307-638-2079
Web: www.therapydogs.com

Delta Society - Pet Partners
875 124th Ave NE, Suite 101, Bellevue, WA 98005 USA.
Email: info@DeltaSociety.org
Web: www.deltasociety.org

Comfort Caring Canines
8135 Lare Street, Philadelphia, PA 19128.
Email: ccc@comfortcaringcanines.org
Web: www.comfortcaringcanines.org/

AUSTRALIA
AWARE Dogs Australia, Inc
PO Box 883, Kuranda, Queensland, 488..
Tel: 07 4093 8152
Web: www.awaredogs.org.au/

Delta Society -- Therapy Dogs
Web: www.deltasociety.com.au

INDEX

ALSO AVAILABLE

Veterinary Advice For Dog Owners is the essential handbook that tells you everything you need to know to keep your dog fit and heathy.

It is a complete home reference guide, covering every aspect of canine health care.

The more you understand about your dog's health and how his body works, the better you are able to care for him. This book will help you...

• Learn how to spot the signs of disease

• Know when to call your vet and seek help

• Feel confident administering first aid

From preventative health care to disease problems and complementary therapies, *Veterinary Advice For Dog Owners* is an essential addition to your bookshelf.

Author Dick Lane has many years' experience as a practising vet. He has a particular interest in assistance dogs and has worked closely with both Guide Dogs For The Blind and Dogs For The Disabled.

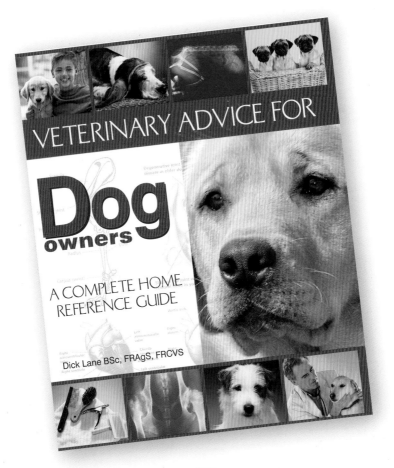